Orange County Scene

A Look At Orange County's Colorful Past

in the Orange County Scene!

Michael C. Kilroy
1-26-97

About This Book

It's not every day a successful businessman publishes a book on local history. But "Orange County Scene" is proof-positive that Joe MacPherson wants to share his love of Orange County.

A third-generation Californian, Mr. MacPherson grew up in the Los Angeles area during the 1930s and '40s. In 1958 he purchased an auto leasing firm in Santa Ana, Calif. that became the launch pad of Team MacPherson, today the largest auto dealership group in Orange County.

During the next three decades Mr. MacPherson, an avid history buff, learned more and more about Orange County's past. In 1995 he decided to publish a column in The Orange County Register that would give the community an inside look at the region's fascinating heritage. The column was titled "Orange County Scene."

The response was overwhelming. Many of the cards and letters asked for a compilation of the "Orange County Scene" columns. Mr. MacPherson heard the message. And in this book, the reader will find selected stories about Orange County's colorful past.

Author Mike Kilroy (left) and Joe MacPherson

Team MacPherson Publishing
CHEVROLET • FORD • INFINITI • TOYOTA • LEASING

COVER PHOTO:
Canoes glide by the Balboa Pavilion in
Newport Bay, circa 1912.

PRINTED IN THE UNITED STATES OF AMERICA
BY
INKWORKS
BERKELEY, CA 94710

ISBN 0-9655832-0-1

LIBRARY OF CONGRESS CATALOG CARD NUMBER: 96-90911

TABLE OF CONTENTS

Orange County Scene

A Look At Orange County's Colorful Past

'Uncle Billy' Spurgeon, Founder of Santa Ana

Santa Ana, the geographical and political center of Orange County, was first laid out by a man 20-feet up a sycamore tree. His name was William Spurgeon, a pioneer settler who literally put the city on the map.

A native of Kentucky, Spurgeon was one miner from the 1849 California Gold Rush who actually did pretty well for himself. He ended up returning to the Midwest and began a successful mercantile business.

After his wife's death in 1867, Spurgeon decided to return to California and start anew. Learning of a growing farm community south of Los Angeles, his goal was to create a centrally located city to serve the local farmers.

When he arrived in what would become Orange County, the mustard grass was so high he could not get a good view of the land. So Spurgeon climbed the sycamore, and saw where he would erect a new town.

On Oct. 27, 1869, Spurgeon paid $594 for 74.25 acres, sharing costs with business partner Maj. Ward Bradford. The two pitched tents for a few months while George Wright of Los Angeles laid out the 24-square-block townsite. The boundaries were First Street to the south, Seventh Street to the north, West (now Broadway) Street to the west and Spurgeon Street to the east.

He named the new city Santa Ana, after the Spanish land grant name for the area, Rancho Santiago de Santa Ana.

As soon as redwood lumber arrived from Northern California, Spurgeon and Bradford erected the town's first building - the Spurgeon Store, which sold sundry items. Spurgeon remarried and made his home in one-half of the building with his new wife, the former Jennie English.

Spurgeon soon became known as "Uncle Billy" to new residents of Santa Ana. One of his contemporaries described him this way:

"The man was not a dreamer. He was a hard-headed, feet-on-the-ground merchant who counted his money carefully, planned logically, treated his children with tender kindness, feared God, but made the most of every opportunity to carry out his plans for the city."

And that he did. A year after founding Santa Ana, Spurgeon decided the city needed to have a stop for a stagecoach. At his own expense, he cut a three-mile long road through the mustard grass and convinced the Wells Fargo stageline to make scheduled stops. He later cut a road several miles north to Anaheim to encourage commerce between the two towns.

A few short months after laying out his city, Spurgeon formed the Spring Street School District. A school opened in January 1870 in a one-room structure Spurgeon supplied himself.

Spurgeon was also one of the original founders of the first church in Santa Ana, the Methodist Episcopal Church South. It was renamed the Spurgeon Memorial Methodist Church after a daughter of Spurgeon's who drowned in the ocean off Laguna Beach.

For decades, Uncle Billy was synonymous with Santa Ana. A visitor from the East recalled in a letter home, "Mr. Spurgeon is postmaster, storekeeper, mayor, alderman, marshal and keeps up a large mercantile establishment where you can purchase everything from a darning needle to a Chicago ham."

With the help of Orange County businessmen James McFadden and James Fruit, Spurgeon formed the Western Development Company to lure the Southern Pacific Railroad to his new town. Competition from the city of Tustin was intense, but the company won the contract.

The coming of the railroad in 1878 marked Santa Ana's emergence as the real commercial center of the county. Farmers would bring their products to town while Spurgeon offered free lunches, banners and music to those who came to Santa Ana considering settling there. His company developed 164 acres in that year alone to make way for the additional businesses and homes.

By the early 1880s the wooden, clapboard buildings were being replaced by the appearance of larger brick structures, a sure sign of Santa Ana's economic prosperity. There were now nearly 100 businesses in town, and new homes were being constructed on a weekly basis.

A Wells Fargo office opened in the new, two-story Spurgeon General Store, with Uncle Billy as agent. A telegraph office was installed, while real estate agents touted the Santa Ana Valley nationwide as "the golden land of milk and honey."

By 1886, Santa Ana was considered by many to be only second in size and importance to Los Angeles. Its citizens called for the city's incorporation, and a subsequent election won that designation. William Spurgeon was named the chairman of the city's original board of trustees.

Rudimentary police and fire departments were formed, and gas mains were laid through the streets and alleys, giving the city its first streetlights. Fine Victorian homes were erected, including the Halladay House, Harmon-McNeil House, Dr. Howe-Waffle House and other elegant structures that survive in the downtown area to this day.

In 1889, Spurgeon and other business leaders were instrumental in forming a separate county from Los Angeles, with Santa Ana as the seat for the new County of Orange. Spurgeon was again elected chairman of the county's board of trustees, and went to work planning the Orange County Courthouse, which was built in 1900.

Spurgeon's namesakes continued to serve the community. William Spurgeon III was a leader in the Boy Scouts, while William IV is a schoolteacher today in the Santa Ana Unified School District.

Spurgeon died in 1915. All his dreams for the city he had envisioned from the sycamore tree years before had come true.

Santa Ana founder William Spurgeon with wife Jennie in front of their first store

JUAN FLORES, THE BADDEST BANDIT OF THE OLD WEST

I always thought stories of the Old West happened in places like Tombstone and Hangman's Gulch. But Orange County has its share of Western lore, too.

More than a century ago, bandits roamed the area stealing cattle and horses and generally terrorizing the ranchos and small towns. By most historical accounts, the most notorious Orange County bandit of all was Juan Flores.

Flores was the 20-year-old black sheep son of a prominent Santa Barbara family who was sent to San Quentin prison for horse-stealing. He soon escaped and fled south.

Flores formed a gang of nearly 50 fugitives into a force he called Los Manillas (The Handcuffs), a band that robbed and terrorized its way to San Juan Capistrano.

The bandits spent two days of hell-raising in the sleepy little town. They amused themselves by taking potshots at a bull's head in the town plaza. When a merchant suggested they stop endangering the citizenry, the Manillas vowed to shoot up the town some more.

Many townspeople fled to the security of the Mission, which was owned at the time by a well-armed rancher. By nightfall, every store and cantina in town was in a shambles.

During that night of Jan. 22, 1857, the gang shot and killed shopkeeper George Pfulgardt as he was making his dinner.

Tradition has it that Flores' sweetheart, Chola Martina, set up the slaying for her outlaw beau. Martina, a dark-eyed beauty known as "La Muchacha de los Sauces" (The Girl of the Willows), called for the shopkeeper at his house.

When Pfulgardt opened the door, Martina lit a cigarette to signal the waiting gunmen. After killing the shopkeeper, the gang ate his dinner and continued shooting up the town.

As luck would have it, the very horses Flores had been sent to prison for stealing had been brought to San Juan from Los Angeles. The freight hauler was Garnet Hardy, one of the brothers from whom Flores had stolen the horses.

The bandit vowed to rob and kill Hardy as revenge for his imprisonment, but a local woman overheard the plot and alerted Hardy, who slipped out of town with the horses.

Hardy reached Don José Sepulveda, owner of the Rancho San Joaquin, whose house stood at the head of Newport Bay. He told the rancher about the murder in San Juan Capistrano.

The next day, Sheriff James Barton arrived at Sepulveda's home with a posse of four men. Over breakfast, Don Jose warned them that they were too few in number to fight the Manillas. But Barton disregarded the advice, and the five mounted up with Hardy to find the outlaw and his gang.

Unknown to the posse, their guns had been tampered with during breakfast. Many believed it was Martina, once again doing misdeeds for her sweetheart.

When the posse reached the site of what is now the Laguna Freeway overpass at the San Diego Freeway, 20 Manillas rode downhill toward them and opened fire. Their guns useless, Barton and three of his deputies were killed. Hardy and two others managed to escape.

Word of the "Barton Massacre" reached Los Angeles. There were calls for a posse to hunt Flores and avenge the death of the popular sheriff.

Three days later a 119-man posse led by General Andres Pico headed south. They found Flores and his gang hiding out in Santiago Canyon. A wild gunfight ensued, and Flores and 10 of his men scrambled up the peak that now bears his name.

Flores sent his horse over the 200-foot bluff on the other side, then slid down himself. Only the bandit and two others escaped. The three were tracked to a cave in what is now Irvine Park and surrendered a few days later.

Flores and his companions were taken to a jail in Olive, but they escaped during the night.

General Pico heard news of the escape and immediately hanged two of the captured Manillas from a sycamore tree. "Here's two that won't be going anywhere," Pico reportedly said at the hanging.

According to accounts of the incident, the two hanged outlaws remained dangling in their nooses for months. Today, the bent sycamore off Santiago Canyon Road from which the outlaws met their fate is known as "Hangman's Tree."

Flores was recaptured four days later in what is now Hollywood, "riding a sorry-looking animal without even a pocket knife to his name," according to one account.

He was brought to Fort Hill in Los Angeles. Before a trial could take place, a mob paid him a visit at his jail cell with no interference from deputies.

On February 24, 1857, he was given "a long hanging and a short funeral," wrote one reporter. As an added touch, Garnet Hardy was given the privilege of adjusting the bandit's noose.

So ended the life and story of Juan Flores, baddest man of the Wild West here in Orange County.

Hangman's Tree in Santiago Canyon where the outlaws met their fate

TUSTIN BLIMP HANGARS - COUNTY'S MASSIVE MARVELS

Standing next to the colossal twin hangars at the Tustin Marine Corps Helicopter Air Station, you feel like you're in the presence of the Eighth Wonder of the World.

That's the kind of awe these structures inspire. Roughly 1,000-feet long, 300-feet wide and 180-feet tall, each hangar could comfortably house six Goodyear blimps, three Matterhorn rides from Disneyland, or even the Queen Mary (minus the front smokestack).

They are purportedly the largest wood-frame structures in the world. Through the years they have become treasured landmarks to many Orange County residents.

The story of the hangars began 54 years ago during World War II. After Japan attacked Pearl Harbor, the U.S. was concerned that the next attack would be along the California coastline.

Both air and sea had to be placed under constant surveillance. While enemy planes could be detected with radar, enemy submarines were a little more difficult to find.

On the Atlantic coast, blimps had been used successfully to stop German U-boat attacks on Allied merchant ships. Navy officials decided to bring the anti-submarine program to the Pacific.

The Navy had one problem - where to house the massive airships. Because of stepped-up ship production, steel was at a premium. Navy engineers and draftsmen were given two months to come up with a solution. They decided to build huge hangars out of wood.

Navy officials found two Pacific Northwest lumber companies that could pre-fabricate sufficient timber to build the hangars. Before shipment, each beam was cut to the correct length and holes were drilled at precise points for installing bolts and fixtures.

The timber was treated with fire-resistant chemicals and shipped to Orange County as well as to Moffett Field Naval Air Station in Northern California where another hangar was being constructed. To accommodate the county's shipment, a special rail spur was extended off the Southern Pacific line to a flat stretch of bean fields in what was then Santa Ana.

Hundreds of workers were brought to the site. Giant concrete pylons were first sunk 150 feet into the ground to anchor the structure. The huge wooden arches, which had been sheathed in galvanized tin to protect them from the elements, were then carefully raised and put in place. Assembling the wood frame took just 60 days.

The engineers added 120-foot high, motorized wooden doors that opened in sections like an accordion along steel rails.

In 1943, the Long Beach Press-Telegram hailed the newly built hangars as "two mighty examples of American ingenuity - the kind that will whip the Axis powers!"

Six blimps, each 100 feet longer than the Goodyear blimp Columbia, were assigned to each hangar. Each blimp's cabin carried six depth charges, a machine gun and crew of nine.

Every morning the helium-filled airships were taken aloft to serve as lookouts for military convoys and commercial ships. Because of their slow speed, low fuel consumption and ability to fly below radar, they were the perfect submarine-busters - if only there were submarines to identify.

It seems that few, if any, enemy submarines were ever spotted. But veteran pilots from the period say the blimps were a deterrent that kept the enemy from venturing into California waters.

Most of the time, the blimps' crews kept busy finding and destroying targets in the ocean. In their spare time they would shoot boars on Catalina Island, or call local fishermen to tell them where schools of fish were running. One year, the local sardine catch rose by several thousand pounds as a result of the blimp pilots' reports.

Even without the enemy around, the operation was a dangerous one. The crew of one blimp was killed when its ship crashed on Catalina Island. A few months later, a 10-man ground crew was electrocuted when a blimp hit a power line. Later, a blimp explosion killed all but one of the nine-man crew.

After the war, the blimps were phased out. At the start of the Korean War in 1951, the Tustin facility was recommissioned as the first Marine helicopter base and has remained so to this day.

Today, one hangar is closed while the other houses the Heavy Marine Helicopter squadron, its offices and parts storage.

Although the twin structures were placed on the National Register of Historic Places in 1975, that protective designation comes at a price. The bolts that hold the giant wood frames together must be tightened each year at a cost of $400,000.

But then I'm sure the Great Pyramids take their share of upkeep, too.

One of the colossal twin hangars at the Tustin Marine Corps Helicopter Air Station

A Museum for Everyone in Heart of County

Once you've taken a tour of the Bowers Museum of Cultural Art in Santa Ana, you can't help but feel lucky to live in Orange County.

Why? Because right in the heart of the county, just a block or two from the Santa Ana Freeway, we can visit one of the finest museums in the country.

Although it re-opened in 1992, many county residents are still unaware of the huge additions to the Bowers. Step inside and there is something magical everywhere you look.

Exhibit after exhibit displays the exotic art of ancient cultures from Africa, the Americas and the Pacific Rim. This is the "primitive" art that museums have overlooked for many years.

You soon realize these pieces are as intriguing as works by well-known Western artists and sculptors. Many of the artworks were religious objects and possess a mysterious aura.

There's also a huge collection of intricate basketry and other art of Native Americans, historical finds such as a conquistador's helmet and gun, paintings by contemporary California artists, an entertaining presentation of county history, and much, much more.

This is a museum for everyone. And the amazing fact is that it can be seen for just $4.50 for adults, $1.50 for children. That's a lot less than the average "shoot-'em up" movie, and probably a lot better for you.

This sophisticated art complex traces its roots to a quiet, retired farm couple who loved to travel and explore historic places.

Charles Bowers was a Missouri native who followed his parents to Santa Ana in 1888 to help till the family's citrus crops. Three years after his first wife's death in 1905, he married Ada Elvira Abbot. He was 64 and Ada was 58.

Charles made some money by developing his parents' farmland, and he and his new wife began traveling around the country. The two developed a fascination with American history, collecting postcards of historic sites on their trips.

Because they mainly kept to themselves, few knew the Bowers well. But E.B. Sprague, a vice president at the First National Bank, used to visit the couple to talk about their investments. He recalled one meeting when the Bowers expressed an interest in preserving Orange County's history.

Sprague suggested establishing a museum, and they apparently liked the idea. In 1924, the Bowers created a trust to create a "fireproof" museum of local history and a permanent meeting site for the county's historical society.

Following Charles' death at age 87 in 1929, and his wife's death in 1931, the deed to the Bowers' land was presented to the City of Santa Ana. The couple's Victorian farmhouse at 20th and Main streets was razed and a mission-style museum was completed in seven months for the princely sum of $78,000.

But it was the Depression era and the city didn't have any museum operating funds, so the museum remained closed. During this time, WPA artists added finishing touches such as ceiling murals and interior decoration. The museum finally opened four years later on February 15, 1936.

Through a special trust created by the Bowers, $2,500 was set aside to erect a fountain on the museum site. Dedicated to Ada Bowers, the fountain features a life-sized statue of Juan Cabrillo, the first European to explore the California coast.

For years the museum employed a single caretaker. The first was Bessie Beth Colter, a persistent local resident who would drive her Ford Model A around the county collecting historic artifacts.

The museum gradually became a "granny's attic" of miscellaneous Indian and Western relics, creating a massive collection of some 70,000 items. Most are in storage to this day.

It wasn't until the early '70s that the museum started to find its focus. That's when the Bowers showed a well-received exhibit of pre-Columbian art. Afterwards, the idea of showcasing cultural art — the early art of non-Western cultures — became the focal point of the museum's future plans.

By 1986, with the increasing scope of the exhibits, educational programs and social functions, it was clear the museum needed to expand. The city formed a Blue Ribbon committee to discuss renovation plans. The committee debated for more than a year before agreeing on a 52,000-square-foot addition.

Renovations began in October 1988. The $12-million project was funded through a Community Redevelopment grant with the aim of establishing Santa Ana as the county's center of arts and culture.

On October 18, 1992, the Bowers re-opened with a gala affair that attracted more than 10,000 well-wishers. Visitors discovered the little local history museum had been transformed into a state-of-the-art facility dedicated to preserving, studying and exhibiting fine art.

A major addition was the largest rotating exhibitions gallery in the West. To date, the gallery has seen more than 30 of the world's finest traveling art exhibits, including a collection of Pre-Columbian gold objects and a display of Amazonian art.

One innovation now copied by others was the installation of a fine restaurant inside the museum itself. The Topaz Cafe features California cuisine and is open for lunch and dinner. On Thursday evenings, patrons can eat a gourmet meal and then tour the museum.

Across from the cafe is the Gallery Store with a menagerie of exotic gift items from around the world you won't find anywhere else.

Two local history rooms preserve the original vision of the Bowers. One features artifacts from the early county ranch families, while another documents the progression of county history to the present.

The museum has been featured in numerous publications, most notably U.S. News and World Report which selected the Bowers as one of nine "must-see" museums in the country.

Bowers Museum in Santa Ana

CHAPMAN UNIVERSITY, OC'S FIRST FOUR-YEAR COLLEGE

Whenever I visit Chapman University in the city of Orange, I think, "This is what a college campus should look like."

There's a long green lawn rolling up to the white pillars of the administration building. Inside are paintings of past college presidents dating back to 1865.

It's a fitting appearance for Orange County's oldest four-year college and largest private university. But I discovered Chapman University's story began beyond the county line, more than 135 years ago in a small town near Berkeley, Calif.

After the California Gold Rush of 1849, the state's population grew enormously. The state government was unprepared for the large influx of people and had made no financial provisions for public education.

Consequently, many religious groups established their own schools. One small group of church people called the Disciples of Christ opened Hesperian College in Woodland, Calif.

Inspired by the ideas of President-elect Abraham Lincoln, the school accepted members of both sexes and all races — a radical concept for the time. Its first class was held at the exact hour of Lincoln's inauguration on March 4, 1861.

By the late 1880s, the California state legislature was beginning to finance public education. As students transferred into the publicly supported schools, private colleges lost tuition; many were forced to close.

In 1896 the Disciples of Christ founded a seminary in Berkeley to train young people for the ministry. The assets of Hesperian were incorporated as part of Berkeley Bible Seminary.

The seminary's population dwindled to fewer than 10 students by 1915. At a church assembly it was decided that its assets should be transferred to a new Disciples of Christ college planned for Los Angeles.

The college was the brain-child of Charles Clark Chapman, an Illinois native who came to the sunny climes of Southern California in 1893 to help his wife battle tuberculosis. He became a successful rancher growing Valencia oranges and shipping them back east for sale during the winter.

In 1912 Chapman donated $50,000 to help build the new college, while members of the Disciples of Christ Church raised another $150,000. Using additional funds from Hesperian, the California Christian College opened in 1920.

Chapman's generosity to the school continued through the Depression. In 1934, the name of the institution was changed to Chapman College in honor of his support.

Never able to afford college as a young man, the rancher and prominent businessman wrote later that the name change was "a happy dream."

During World War II, the Navy commandeered the Chapman College site in Los Angeles for an engineering school. Whittier College agreed to share its facilities with Chapman, and students began classes there in September 1942.

Student enrollment grew rapidly following the war. President George Reeves decided the college needed room to expand. When he heard the Orange Unified School District planned to build a new high school, he offered to purchase the old campus.

So in 1954 Chapman College moved south to become the first four-year accredited college in Orange County.

The college settled into the historic buildings of the former Orange Union High School on Glassell Avenue. Opened in 1904, the neo-classical architecture is one of the few remaining examples of the style in Southern California. Today, five of the campus buildings are part of the National Register of Historic Places.

In the '60s, Chapman became famous for its World Campus Afloat, where students could take classes onboard a ship sailing around the globe. Although the ship was sold in the '70s, students still have the opportunity to book passage on it for a semester.

In 1991, Chapman officially became a university. The campus is open to students of all faiths. About 100 of the 3,200 student enrollment at the Orange campus are members of the Disciples of Christ Church.

Five schools and a liberal arts college make up the university today, including a law school that opened in 1994. That same year the school started a football program and finished with a winning debut season.

Next on the agenda for Chapman are plans for a chapel on the campus grounds. The chapel will be a place of worship for all denominations. Spectacular drawings have already been rendered by famed chapel architect E.F. Jones.

The chapel, like the university itself, should be a fine complement to the surrounding community and the county at large.

The Chapman College campus when it was Orange Union High School

FENDER, THE GUITAR-MAKER WHO SHOOK THE WORLD

Perhaps no music in this century has had more of an impact on American culture and the world-at-large than rock 'n' roll.

What may surprise many Orange Countians is that a key figure in the music's development was a lifelong resident of Fullerton.

His name was Leo Fender and most music historians agree that rock 'n' roll, and the contemporary style of other musical genres such as country-western and R&B, would have been impossible without him.

Fender is credited with inventing the modern electric guitar. Before him, guitars were either "hollow-bodies" that couldn't be played loud without shrieks of feedback, or were clumsy "lap-style" instruments that required guitarists to perform sitting down.

A self-described "tinkerer," Fender developed the first solid-body guitars that were cheap, easy-to-play and improved the range of sounds and textures an electric guitar could make.

His signature model, the Stratocaster, became the guitar of choice for generations of rock 'n' rollers, from Buddy Holly and the Beach Boys, to Jimi Hendrix and Eric Clapton, to Bruce Springsteen and Nirvana.

No less a rock legend than Keith Richards of the Rolling Stones once said, "Thank God for Leo Fender, who makes these instruments for us to play."

Fender was born on a small farm in Anaheim on Aug. 10, 1909. He had no formal education after high school, and lost his Highway Department job during the Depression. With a knack for fixing electronic gadgetry, Fender opened a small radio repair shop in 1935.

In his spare time, Fender began to repair the primitive electric guitars and amplifiers used by local country-western acts. Fender, who never played the guitar, loved country music and enjoyed helping musicians find a better sound.

By the mid-1940s the radio repairman was working on ideas to improve their guitars. From his "tinkering" he created a prototype that featured a better pick-up, tuning pegs, frets and guitar neck. It was the world's first usable solid-body electric guitar in the standard Spanish style.

He called it the Broadcaster, later discovering a competing musical instruments manufacturer already had patented the name for their drum kit. Fender, mindful of the new medium of television, renamed the guitar the Telecaster.

Released in 1948, the Telecaster was heralded by guitarists from every musical genre — jazz, Big Band, rhythm and blues and country — as a major innovation. It gave guitarists the freedom to play loud enough to be heard and even dominate the sound when needed.

Fender followed up with the Precision Bass guitar in 1951, another musical milestone. It was the first electric alternative to the old acoustic-style, stand-up bass.

With a fast-growing company, Fender had to move out of the small brick building on Pomona Avenue near the Fullerton train station (a parking structure sits at the site today). In 1953 he relocated to a permanent home at Raymond Avenue and Valencia Drive.

Success didn't slow Fender's creativity and vision, however. In 1954 he introduced his masterpiece, the Stratocaster.

While developing "the Strat," as it became known by musicians, Fender spoke with guitarists about what they wanted in an instrument. He incorporated their ideas and added many of his own. The result was an instrument that many still consider to be the perfect electric guitar.

It quickly became a standard in the music industry. Brightly colored with a graceful, ergonomic design, the Stratocaster was instantly recognizable on stages around the world.

The guitar featured a fluid sound never before heard from an electric guitar. A few of its innovations included tone controls, access to more of the fret board to reach higher notes, and a tremolo bar for sound effects.

To early rock musicians the guitar was a godsend. With the Strat priced as low as $75, rockers everywhere now had access to an affordable, high-quality electric guitar. Four- and five-piece rock groups could now have a sound as full as the Big Bands.

Coming from another generation, Fender never really liked the new music, but that didn't stop him from helping local rock musicians such as Dick Dale continue to improve their sound.

Sales of his products grew from $100,000 in 1953 to $11 million just 10 years later. Never one to rest on his laurels, Fender also designed amplifiers that included pioneering features such as tone controls and reverb.

Inevitably, conglomerates came to the Fullerton factory looking to buy the company. In 1964, with Fender in poor health at the time, CBS won the bidding war and purchased the firm for $13 million.

CBS, however, didn't have an inkling how to build electric guitars and the quality of Fender Instruments' products suffered. For years the only Fender guitars real musicians would play were "pre-CBS."

Disappointed in what CBS was doing, Fender returned to guitar-making in the 1970s. He started the Music Man company with some of his old employees. When that fell apart due to differences with company executives, he re-emerged with another guitar company called G&L during the '80s.

While never matching his early innovations, Fender had a lot to be proud of. He had more guitar patents than all U.S. guitar manufacturers combined, had started a company which is today the largest producer of electric guitars, and was the creator of a musical icon — the Stratocaster.

Ironically, for all his success, Fender lived virtually unknown in his hometown of Fullerton until his death in 1991. The next year he was inducted into the Rock 'n' Roll Hall of Fame.

Leo Fender in 1954 with a punch press used to produce the first Stratocasters

MUSEUM IN BUENA PARK PRESERVES FOSSIL RECORD

Most people in Orange County know about the big attractions in Buena Park — Knott's Berry Farm, Movieland Wax Museum and Medieval Times.

Recently, though, I discovered the city has the only museum in Orange County dedicated to preserving and displaying area fossils.

Located inside Ralph B. Clark Regional Park, it's called the Interpretive Center. The facility offers a fascinating glimpse into the county's ancient past.

According to paleontologist Lisa Babilonia-Jones, most of the center's fossils were excavated from two nearby "rock units." The marine rock unit, found just across the street from the park, was a beach 1.5-million years ago. Here workers find fossils of what you may expect to find on a beach — shells, fish bones and shark teeth.

Inside the park are marshland rock units named Elephant Hill and Camel Hill. Excavations have uncovered fossils of the many large mammals that once roamed the area 400,000 to 500,000 years ago.

These include bones and teeth from mammoths, giant ground sloths, large tapirs, saber-toothed cats, horses and llama-like camels.

There are skeletal reconstructions and illustrations in the center that give you a sense of what these animals must have looked like.

The giant sloth skeleton, for instance, stands about seven-feet tall and has large claws for ripping tree branches. The tapir appears to be an oversized pig. And the saber-toothed cat looks as ferocious in skeleton as it must have when it lived.

The stories accompanying the exhibits are informative. For instance, did you know the first camels originated in North America? Some traveled south and eventually became llamas, while others traveled to Asia and the Middle East.

Horses were plentiful in the area, too, but disappeared some 10,000 years ago. Nobody is certain why they died out, but they didn't return until Europeans brought them to these shores 400 years ago.

I also didn't realize some of the animals we find in today's county wilderness have been with us for a long time.

There was once a saber-toothed opossum that roamed the area 40,000 years before his less menacing cousin. And coyotes have been chasing rabbits here for more than 70,000 years.

The park has one of the richest fossil deposits in the state. Babilonia-Jones says, "I could be happy excavating in the park for the next 20 years because of all the new species we find here."

The fossils were first discovered when Caltrans began excavating sand and gravel for construction of the Santa Ana and Riverside freeways during the '50s and '60s. Then called the Emery Borrow Pit, workers at the site collected fossils as curiosities.

In 1969, though, the L.A. County Museum of Natural History learned of the site and began excavations. During the next four years more than 4,000 fossils were recovered.

Because of public demand for the site's preservation, the County of Orange acquired the property in 1974. The park was built five years later while the 5,400-square-foot Interpretive Center opened in 1988.

The center's current featured exhibit is one of the most complete fossil skeletons of a prehistoric whale ever found.

Nicknamed "Joaquin," it was discovered two years ago during construction of the Transportation Corridor in Laguna Niguel.

The 27-foot-long, 9-million-year-old skeleton of the extinct species of baleen whale is displayed just as it was found in the earth.

An accompanying illustration depicts the deepwater channel that existed between the Saddleback Mountains and Laguna Niguel Island. It was in this channel the whale died, turned belly up, and sunk into the muddy sea floor.

The center is also a research facility, and has a glass-walled lab where visitors can watch fossil specimens being prepared by staff and volunteers. All finds are stored and catalogued so scientists from other parts of the country can easily compare and contrast fossils.

There are many things of interest to kids at the center, and school tours are conducted daily. One of the displays is a model of Tyrannosaurus Rex that isn't too accurate. It once advertised a pest control company.

Those who take the group tour have the opportunity to go into the field to discover fossils themselves. Although any finds must remain at the park, the fossil-hunting expedition is a unique experience.

A giant sloth that roamed the county a half-million years ago

The Story of the El Toro Marine Corps Air Base

Despite the roar of F-15 fighter jets over the skies of Orange County and the annual air show, the El Toro Marine Corps Air Station has been a relatively quiet county resident the past 54 years.

Yet no site in the county has been home to so much U.S. history. Through the years, the largest Marine air station on the West Coast has seen aerial innovations, decorated combat wings, presidential visits, the landing of Vietnamese refugees, and much more.

With the 6,200-acre base set to close in the next few years and a debate raging over what will become of the site, this is a good time to trace its history and impact on the county.

The military first considered Orange County as a site for an air station in 1928. That year Rear Admiral W.A. Moffett, chief of naval aviation, landed at Eddie Martin Airport (now John Wayne Airport). Moffett spoke with rancher James Irvine about purchasing two large lima bean fields — one in El Toro and another in what would become the city of Tustin.

Much to Irvine's relief, the Navy decided on a site in Northern California. The rancher did not want to lose his most productive bean fields. But 14 years later, following the attack on Pearl Harbor, Marine Corps Aviation came knocking on Mr. Irvine's door.

Acting on the advice of Admiral Moffett, Col. William Fox inquired about the parcels of land the Navy had reviewed earlier. Irvine, attempting to keep his prime farm land, tried offering other sites on his vast ranch for one-dollar a year.

The Marines, however, wanted the bean field in El Toro. It was perfect for an air station — the field sat in a shallow valley and was almost fog-free, the main Santa Fe Railroad line ran past it, and it was a short distance from Camp Pendleton, the Marine infantry training base.

In early 1942 the Marines paid Irvine $100,000 for nearly 4,000 acres, which included land set aside to build the lighter-than-air ship base in Tustin. Irvine used the money from the sale to purchase an 82,000-acre ranch in Montana.

While Irvine may not have been happy about the sale, County of Orange officials were ecstatic. They realized the Marine base would help transform the county from a farming region to a residential and industrial center in the years to come.

Construction of MCAS El Toro began on Aug. 3, 1942 and Commanding Officer Col. Theodore Millard was sent to oversee the work. Upon his arrival the colonel learned 30 Marines, the first ever assigned to the base, were at the train station three miles away.

No military transportation had been arranged, so Col. Millard drove his own private vehicle back and forth over the next few hours until all the men were on site. Since no barracks had been built as yet, the Marines were housed in bunkhouses on the Irvine Ranch.

By December 1942 the airplane runways, taxiways and run-up areas were completed, and by January the first barracks were finished.

El Toro was officially commissioned on St. Patrick's Day, March 17, 1943 in a ceremony complete with parade, flag-raising and fly-over of the "Douglas Dauntless" dive bombers. Tragedy marred the event when an F-4 Wildcat crashed while attempting a slow roll above the crowds and the young pilot was killed.

Later that year base officials asked Walt Disney to design an insignia. Disney, a former leatherneck himself, presented the base with a design of a snarling red bull with Marine Corps emblem and wings (El Toro means "the bull" in Spanish). He sold the copyright for $1 and "The Flying Bull" emblem has been seen the world over wherever El Toro Marines have flown.

One year after its groundbreaking, 7,000 military personnel and 550 civilians were working on the base. The first squadron assigned to El Toro was VMF-113, led by Maj. "Doc" Everton. Fresh from combat duty against Japan, the squadron served as instructors to new aviation recruits.

El Toro's mission of preparing pilots for combat was a critical one for the Pacific theater during World War II. Many of the pilots trained at the base became top aces and leaders in Marine Corps aviation. One of the pilots was John Glenn, who later became America's first man in orbit.

A strange footnote to the war years is that Trabuco Road once crossed directly through the base.

The road was the only way residents of the town of El Toro could get to central and north Orange County. Civilian automobiles were checked at the main gate and then allowed to continue through the base. Traffic lights were installed at the major runways for the cars and Marine Corps pilots.

With the surrender of Japan in 1945, the future of the air station was in serious doubt. The Santa Ana Army Air Base, as well as a half-dozen other West Coast bases, were decommissioned.

A cost-conscious Congress considered turning MCAS El Toro back into a bean field in 1949. However, with tensions rising between the U.S. and the Soviets, Congress changed its mind. The outbreak of the Korean War in 1950 sealed the decision to maintain the base for a long time to come.

Opening ceremonies for the El Toro Marine Corps Air Station on March 17, 1943

GOSPEL SWAMP - DAYS OF FIRE AND BRIMSTONE

There is no more modest place of worship in all Orange County than the Greenville Country Church in Santa Ana, yet no church besides Mission San Juan Capistrano has a longer history.

The white, A-frame wood structure is located on a small stretch of farmland near the South Coast Plaza mall. The day I visited the church, the sun's rays were breaking through the clouds just above the steeple, creating a heavenly sight.

A plaque outside the church entrance says the church was built in 1876, making it the oldest Protestant church in the county. Through the years, it has been the site of services for five denominations — Methodist, Presbyterian, Baptist, Russian Orthodox and Independent Evangelist.

The church began in the long-forgotten mists of Gospel Swamp.

In 1828, the Santa Ana River overflowed its banks once again, creating a 30,000-acre marshland that stretched from southwest Santa Ana to the ocean at Huntington Beach.

It was considered a wasteland by most 19th-century county farmers until a few hardy souls began dredging away the muck around 1870. Most of these families attempting to reclaim the swamp were farmers who had moved from the South and shared a strict work ethic and a fundamentalist Christian faith.

Beneath the swampland the farmers discovered some of the most fertile soil in the state. On small stretches of cleared land, these resourceful men and women were able to grow bumper crops of celery, lima beans, corn and other vegetables.

But the religious people scattered throughout the giant marshland had no church. So it was during this time itinerant preachers began holding revival meetings under huge tents for the farming families. The abundant free land, artesian wells and shade made it a cool, pleasant camping ground for the faithful.

A Baptist minister named Isaac Hickey was one of the early settlers in the area and held the first of what would be many fire-and-brimstone revival meetings.

A story that has been passed down for generations claims that a local farm boy, required by his parents to attend the lengthy revival meetings, complained, "All we've got down here is gospel and swamp."

The "Gospel Swamp" name gained popularity after it was later used in a story by the now-defunct Anaheim Gazette. Those who lived in the cities of Santa Ana and Anaheim used the term as a put-down of the marshland's less refined inhabitants.

But the land was good to the farmers, with one preacher calling Gospel Swamp a "veritable Egypt" during one harvest. The fertility of the soil was phenomenal, yielding as much as 125 bushels of corn per acre. Pumpkins grew so large (some weighing more than 100 pounds apiece) it was said a child could cross an entire field of them without ever touching the ground.

The farmers got help selling their crops when a flat-bottomed boat called the Vaquero began making periodic stops in Newport Bay. The Vaquero took loads of vegetables to markets in Los Angeles and San Diego.

In 1876 William Tedford, a successful Gospel Swamp farmer, decided it was time for a church to be built in the area. He donated land at the edge of the marshland and the community helped build the structure from redwood a year later.

It was called the Methodist Episcopal Church South and became a stop for a traveling minister named P.O. Clayton. Services were also conducted by Rev. Hickey and his Baptist congregation and by the Presbyterians living nearby.

In 1880 a parsonage was erected to house a pastor and his family. One of the early pastors was C.E. Knott, father of Knott's Berry Farm founder Walter Knott. More than 50 pastors have served the church through-out the years.

During the 1900s the church became known as the Old Newport Church, but when a young pastor who was to preach on Sunday was directed to Newport Beach instead, the congregation decided to change the name.

For years, those from the cities had called the residents in the area "green hicks," so the church members agreed on the name Greenville Country Church, turning the name into a badge of honor.

The great marshland gradually disappeared to development, but somehow the church remained. In 1952, when the Methodists planned to raze the church, a local Christian evangelist congregation raised funds and purchased the property.

The preacher's first sermon following the change of hands was titled "Destroy Not the Landmarks Your Forefathers Built."

The church looks like it would be right at home in the Ozarks instead of Orange County. The interior has retained much of its 1870s character, with the original church pews, pulpit, pot-bellied stove and organ. A bell tower was added in 1960 to call in children for Sunday school.

While a larger church was built next door by the Independent Evangelists in the 1960s, the original Greenville Country Church is still used for weddings and other special occasions. A small group of Russian Orthodox faithful also conduct services during the week.

Today the little white church stands as a humble monument to the Gospel Swamp farmers and those in later years who refused to let their faith die.

A Gospel Swamp family attends a revival meeting in the early 1900s.

GLENN MARTIN - FIRST TO FLY THE COUNTY'S SKIES

With its blue skies and miles of farmland tailor-made for soft landings, Orange County was once a hotbed for those daring young men and their flying machines in the early 20th century.

Two of the more successful pioneer pilots were Glenn Martin and Eddie Martin. They shared the same last name, but they were related only in their passion for flight.

Both men's early tinkering with flying machines resulted in two modern-day companies — Martin Aviation in Irvine, founded by Eddie, and Martin-Marietta, now part of Lockheed, founded by Glenn.

Glenn Martin was the county's original aviator. He worked as a salesman in his dad's Santa Ana Ford dealership by day, and was a well-known motorcycle enthusiast in his spare time. Glenn held the record of traveling the dirt roads from Santa Ana to San Juan Capistrano in 26 minutes.

When he wasn't racing motorcycles, the young Martin built flying contraptions in his backyard. His first gliders soared over the local farms. When he caught wind of the Wright Brothers aerial feat in 1903, Glenn Martin set about mimicking their historic motorized flight.

Using a rebuilt Ford engine, Martin's first creation never got airborne. With that expensive failure, he lost his dad's support for his new-found hobby, but his mother continued to encourage his aviation dreams.

He wrote the Wright Brothers, asking permission to build a plane using their patents. They agreed, and Martin rented a vacant downtown Santa Ana church and painted over the windows to maintain secrecy.

The spruce and bamboo contraption that he built was powered by a 15-horsepower Ford engine. When he was finished, his mother and two helpers pushed it

down a dirt road to a bean field owned by James Irvine II. The pioneer pilot offered the rancher the honor of being his first passenger, but Irvine declined.

At dawn on Aug. 1, 1909 Martin accomplished his first flight. Clearing the lima beans at an altitude of eight feet, the determined young man remained airborne for all of 12 seconds and covered 100 feet.

He had put himself in the record books. With that flight, Glenn Martin became only the third person in the U.S. to fly a powered heavier-than-air machine. His plane was also the first ever to be built and flown in California.

News of his feat reached the public and the Santa Ana Chamber of Commerce began to promote exhibitions of the plane and assisted in raising funds for the new aviator.

Martin was soon known as "The Flying Fool from Santa Ana" and he began performing barnstorming demonstrations. He always wore a business suit, white shirt, tie, hat and gold-rimmed glasses — the Harold Lloyd of early pilots. When he got a little more respect for his flying, his nickname was changed to "The Flying Dude."

Martin's goal was to fly over waterways, and he designed a bi-plane equipped with pontoons for landing on both water and land. He received permission from developer William Collins to use a strip of his Balboa peninsula property as a launching site for the new plane.

On a foggy morning in May 1912, Martin took off over the ocean. The overcast weather forced him to climb to an unprecedented altitude of 4,000 feet. Thirty-seven minutes later, he lowered his hydroplane through a break in the clouds and landed in the surf off Catalina Island. He then taxied onto the beach.

Pausing only long enough to eat a snack and re-fuel the plane, Martin headed back for the mainland, landing at Balboa again. He had set two world records: the longest over-water flight with a 79-minute duration and the fastest over-water flight at an average 53 mph.

His plane was also the first to ever land at Catalina

— and he even carried the island's first air mail back to the mainland.

Wanting to profit from his innovations, the flyer started the Glenn L. Martin Co., manufacturing planes in a vacant fruit cannery in Santa Ana.

The firm later moved to Los Angeles, then to Cleveland and Baltimore, eventually becoming the Martin-Marietta Corp. It was later purchased by aerospace giant Lockheed.

In the 1930s the company produced the China Clipper flying boat, the first commercial plane capable of crossing an ocean.

Other highlights in Martin's career included designing commercial planes with Orville Wright and playing the role of pilot in a Mary Pickford movie. He returned to Orange County in 1937 to commemorate the 25th anniversary of his history-making channel flight. He piloted one of his amphibious Clippers over the same route from Balboa to Catalina.

Pioneer aviator Glenn Martin in his first flying machine, circa 1911

EDDIE MARTIN, FATHER OF ORANGE COUNTY AVIATION

When you look at the state-of-the-art John Wayne Airport today, it's hard to imagine that its roots can be traced to a silk-scarfed aviator from the 1920s named Eddie Martin.

To many, Martin is synonymous with Orange County aviation history. He founded the county's first airport, taught thousands how to fly and helped bring about the local enthusiasm for flight which continues to this day.

Eddie Martin arrived in Orange County in a covered wagon in 1903, the year the Wright Brothers made their historic Kitty Hawk flight. His family had moved from Riverside County to start a farm in Fountain Valley.

As a youngster, Martin's first interest was automobiles and he dreamt of a career as a race car driver. But his dreams changed when he saw his first plane at the old Santa Ana Race Track in 1912.

The occasion was a race between aviator Lincoln Beachey's airplane and auto racer Barney Oldfield's Fiat. Oldfield's car beat the plane around the one-mile oval track, but young Martin had seen enough. He was going to fly.

His first flight had to wait until 1921 when Martin took a few lessons from two former Army pilots in a Lincoln Standard J-1 bi-plane. But the two fliers demolished the plane in a Northern California crash and Martin had to wait to fly again.

While working as a mechanic for a Santa Ana auto dealership in 1923, Martin heard of a local barnstorming pilot named "Ace" Bougoneur. The pilot was earning a living flying passengers in a Curtiss JN-4 (Jenny) World War I trainer.

Martin's brother Johnny, a salesman at the dealership, persuaded his boss to swap a car for the plane and then re-sell the aircraft to Eddie for $700. Eddie's flying career had begun.

To attract passengers, Eddie moved the airplane to an open field on the Irvine Ranch at the intersection of Main Street and Newport Avenue.

Despite his inexperience, Martin managed to take off and land the plane safely with his first passengers on-board. The flights became a lucrative weekend business.

During one of these early flights Martin landed on the family ranch. It was the first time his father learned of his son's interest in aviation.

A few weeks later Martin got the courage to tell the Irvine family about his trespassing on their land. Rancher James Irvine was already aware of the unauthorized airport, and, instead of removing the young aviator, he offered him a five-year lease on the 80-acre property.

So officially began the Eddie Martin Airport and Flying School, the first permanent airport in the county.

The flying business boomed in the '20s. Eddie launched the Santa Ana Air Club, which included many of his students, both men and women.

"Orange County was the ideal place in the U.S. to fly and teach students," Martin once said. "There was a gentle breeze from the southwest and you could set down anywhere if you had to — there were no legal limitations on aviation."

The airport got its first hangar in 1926, which Martin traded for his motorcycle. He made air cargo history when he delivered the cycle to the new owner by air.

In 1927 Eddie bought a Nieuport 28, a modified French World War I fighter. He often did stunts with the plane over Santa Ana to drum up business and entered it in local air races.

Later that year the Santa Ana Register hired the Martin operation to deliver its sport edition to the coastal communities from Huntington Beach to San Clemente. But it failed to stimulate circulation and the stunt was discontinued after three weeks.

His aviation business continued to grow and the airport became a major stop-over for pilots coming to Southern California. In 1928, one of those pilots was Charles Lindbergh who needed directions to an aircraft company in Midway City.

Other famous aviators visiting the airport included Howard Hughes in 1935, who took off from the Martin strip but crash-landed in an Irvine bean field. Hughes set a new world speed record that day of 352 mph. Among the spectators was Amelia Earhart.

By 1937 both Martin's brothers, Johnny and Floyd, had joined Eddie in the airport business. Their partnership was the basis for present-day Martin Aviation in Santa Ana.

In 1939 the County of Orange was planning to build its own airport and extend Main Street, essentially destroying the Martins' airport. But the Irvines came to the rescue. The family offered the county a new airport site with the stipulation of a 17-year lease for the Martins.

The county agreed and on Sept. 1, 1941 the new Orange County Airport opened for business with a 2,500-foot paved runway, taxi strip, administration building and hangar for Martin Aviation.

But the new field had a short life. The military commandeered it for World War II flight operations and banned civilian flying within 150 miles of the coast. Eddie spent the war years working as a test pilot for Lockheed Aircraft in Burbank.

After the war, Eddie decided he'd had enough of commercial flying and turned his focus toward real estate and automobiles. He would make periodic visits to Martin Aviation, which was still by managed by his brothers.

Though Martin Aviation was sold in 1963, Eddie remained the unofficial chairman emeritus of the firm. He donated many of his personal mementos, including his original pilot's license signed by Orville Wright, to a museum established at the company's headquarters.

A plaque bearing Martin's likeness was dedicated Feb. 16, 1989 during ceremonies at the John Wayne Airport. Martin died a year later, following a lengthy illness.

So the next time you see a jet landing at the John Wayne Airport, remember it all began with an enterprising young aviator with goggles and a dream.

Eddie Martin with his favorite plane, the Nieuport 28, at Martin Airport

THE BITTERSWEET STORY OF THE HOLLY SUGAR FACTORY

When you're a kid, sugar is like gold. And that's why I remember the Holly Sugar Factory off the Newport Freeway.

During the summer, I could smell the sweet aroma emanating from the factory's doors. I imagined that inside it looked like the movie "Willie Wonka and the Chocolate Factory." It seemed like the best place anyone could work.

Well, I grew up and, unfortunately, the giant yellow-brick factory was torn down. But I am reminded of it every time I pass Dyer Road and see the Windsor Suites Hotel that now stands at the site.

Like a lot of things in Orange County, the factory's story began with the Irvine ranch family. The Irvines once owned thousands of acres of sugar beet fields. When James Irvine couldn't get the price he wanted from a local sugar processor, he started the Santa Ana Cooperative Sugar Company to build a sugar factory for his and other local farmers' beets.

The Dyer Company of Cincinnati was brought in to design and construct the factory, hence the name Dyer Road. (A little historical sidenote: Company founder E.H. Dyer began this country's first sugar processing plant in 1879.)

Completed in 1911, the three-story factory was built almost exclusively out of bricks and was located on a 45-acre site, taking up an entire city block.

The factory was designed to process six hundred tons of beets daily. To keep it busy operating, the cooperative purchased thousands of acres of additional land and leased it to other sugar beet farmers.

By World War I, with sugar factories in Santa Ana, Anaheim, Huntington Beach and Los Alamitos, Orange County was producing 100,000 tons of sugar beets a year, and a fifth of the nation's processed sugar.

In 1918, the Santa Ana Cooperative sold the factory to the Holly Sugar Company. Holly Sugar took over processing the beets for the Irvine ranch and continued to do so for decades afterwards.

Supplying the factory with enough beets to make it a profitable operation was not an easy task for farmers. A ton of beets only produced about 275 pounds of refined sugar.

To grow the needed tonnage, the beet fields demanded heavy fertilization and deep plowing — about 14 inches into the ground, or double that of most other crops.

When the beets grew to about two pounds, the harvesting and processing began and would not end for four to six months. The "sugarmen" often worked more than 100 12-hour days in a row until the harvest was over.

First the beets were plowed and "topped" — cutting off the top part of the beet by hand where there was little sugar. The tops were saved for cattle feed.

The beets arrived at the factory by railroad car. Samples were taken and farmers were paid a standard price per ton for a given sugar content. If there was more sugar content than usual, the price, and their profits, went up.

The beets were dumped into V-shaped bins and gradually released into a water-filled flume to be floated into the factory. The water helped loosen the dirt before the beets went in a washer.

Then the beets were cut into shoestring pieces. The pieces fell through a chute into cylinders and cooked in near-boiling water until the sugar had been extracted from the pulp.

The pulp was set aside, and the sugar-laden water was put through chemical treatments, filters and a centrifuge before the granulated sugar you find on your table was produced. The pulp was mixed with molasses, another by-product of the granulating process, and sold for cattle feed.

During the '20s, the other county sugar factories closed when nematode attacks depleted usable crops.

The parasitic worm infestation was caused by farmers planting beets in the same fields year after year.

Yet the Holly Sugar Factory somehow survived for decades, getting its beets by railroad car from Riverside and San Bernardino counties. In the '60s, after Castro took control of Cuba and its sugar fields, the factory saw another boom time in production.

In 1973 the last sugar beets were harvested in Orange County on the Irvine ranch. Freight prices had also escalated, causing the plant to operate in the red.

Faced with huge losses, the Holly factory shut down its beet processing and turned to producing corn syrup blends for soft drinks, catsup, salad dressing and other food products.

In 1979, the factory also became a sugar cane refinery. Ships from the Philippines and South America brought raw sugar to Long Beach Harbor where it was shipped by rail to the Holly plant.

But the changes still couldn't make the plant profitable. Three years later, the Holly Sugar Factory shut its doors.

For a time Holly tried to find a developer who would purchase the building and renovate it. But because of the high cost of retro-fitting the building for earthquakes, no investors were interested.

County historical societies attempted to stop the plant's demolition. Many considered the structure to be as important to local history as the San Juan Capistrano Mission or the Old Santa Ana Courthouse.

But the factory's time had passed. And in 1983 the county's reminder of a sweeter time was destroyed.

The yellow-brick Holly Sugar Factory was a distinctive county landmark for 72 years.

ORANGE COUNTY: HOME TO HOLLYWOOD MOVIES

Through the years Orange County has been the backdrop for hundreds of movies, coinciding with the emergence of Hollywood as the film capital of the world.

Pharaoh's chariots have driven Moses and the Israelites to the very edge of the Pacific Ocean in Seal Beach, a bloody battle from World War I raged across an open field in Corona del Mar, the Hindenburg dirigible exploded in flames in Tustin...

Early movie producers were drawn to the county's varying locales, from shimmering beaches to rugged canyons and spacious fields. And it was all just a short train or auto trip from Hollywood.

According to historian Jim Sleeper, the first movie ever filmed here was a one-reeler by D.W. Griffith in 1910 called "The Two Brothers." Shot in and around Mission San Juan Capistrano, one of its minor players was Mary Pickford, who eventually found her way to stardom.

Griffith's effort launched a movie-making rush, with more than 500 films made in Orange County over the next 20 years, drawing some of the biggest names of the silent movie era.

In the 1917 version of "Cleopatra" for instance, Upper Newport Bay served as the coast of Greece with dark-eyed beauty Theda Bara cast as the queen aboard her floating royal chamber.

Dashing Douglas Fairbanks went to the expense of building a French fort off the Upper Bay for "The Three Musketeers" in 1921, the movie which forever set the style for swash-bucklers.

The top matinee idol of the era, Rudolph Valentino, starred in the 1921 sea saga "Moran of the Lady Letty," shot off Balboa and Pirate's Cove in Corona del Mar.

But it was Buster Keaton who used Orange County most in the 1920s, including his classic "The Navigator" featuring the great stone-faced comic wrestling with an octopus in Newport Bay and meeting cannibals on Balboa Island. Another great silent-era comic, Mack Senett, regularly filmed his Keystone Kops and bathing beauties in Balboa and other beachside sites.

Cecil B. DeMille, the director of celluloid epics, used Seal Beach as the setting for the Sinai in his 1923 epic, "The Ten Commandments."

One Oscar-winning movie was shot in Orange County at the onset of the talkies — director Lewis Milestone's masterpiece "All Quiet on the Western Front." The pastoral hills of sagebrush in Corona del Mar and Newport Beach were transformed into a World War I battlefield with trenches, barbed wire and hundreds of soldiers.

The county's movie rush slowed in the late '20s and early '30s when the first talkies appeared. Because of technical reasons, most had to be shot in studios, ruling out location shots.

By the mid-30s, movies were again being filmed along the county's beaches, including the pirate classic "Captain Blood" in 1935 that jump-started Errol Flynn's career, and the original "A Star is Born" in 1937 with Frederic March and Janet Gaynor.

Ronald Reagan showed up here in 1942 to film in the farm fields of Garden Grove for "Juke Girl" with Ann Sheridan. Numerous other productions were shot in the rustic landscape of Irvine Park, including the ghostly comedy "Topper" with Cary Grant in 1937 and the canine tear-jerker "Lassie Come Home."

Even as rapid growth began to erode much of Orange County's natural landscape, movie-makers still found special sites they needed a short distance away.

James Dean's death-defying "chicken" race in the 1954 classic "Rebel Without a Cause" was filmed on a bluff at Dana Point, while some of the wild plane stunts in the 1963 comedy "It's a Mad, Mad, Mad, Mad World" were shot in the Laguna Canyon area.

In 1972, the UC Irvine campus and its starkly futuristic buildings were the main setting for the simian sequel, "Conquest of the Planet of the Apes."

One of the most spectacular scenes ever shot in the county was the simulation of the Hindenburg dirigible disaster. Shot for a 1975 movie starring George C. Scott, a mock-up of the dirigible was engulfed in flames near the mammoth World War II blimp hangars at the Tustin Marine Corps Air Station.

Perhaps the most recognizable county landmark in film after film is the Old County Courthouse in Santa Ana. The red sandstone landmark possesses a turn-of-the-century ambiance and unusually good acoustics for movie sound.

Among the many productions that have used the second floor's main courtroom as a setting were: "Compulsion" (1959) with Orson Welles as Clarence Darrow; "Norma Rae" (1979) with Sally Field; "Gideon's Trumpet" (1980) with Henry Fonda; and "Frances" (1982) with Jessica Lange.

More recent films shot around the county have included Albert Brooks' after-life comedy "Defending Your Life" (1992), the Disney hockey sequel "Mighty Ducks II" (1993); Arnold Schwarzenegger's "Kindergarten Cop" (1993); and "Clear and Present Danger" (1994) with Harrison Ford.

The latest film to feature local sites is the new Tom Hanks' film "That Thing You Do." The movie's setting of downtown Erie, Penn. in the mid-1960s is actually the Orange Plaza. Hanks and a film crew spent a few weeks in Orange last year shooting scenes for the movie.

Ironically, with all the movies made here over the years, Orange County is almost always a stand-in for other locations. Very few films have actually had Orange County as its setting.

A TV production crew did film some scenes for "Laguna Heat" a few years ago, the murder-detective story by county resident T. Jefferson Parker. However, most of the movie's scenes were shot in Los Angeles, standing in for Orange County.

That's show business, I guess.

A 1920s movie production crew takes a break at Laguna Beach.

ALL ABOARD! THE STORY OF OC'S RAILROADS

Growing up near an orange packing plant in Orange, I could often hear the plaintive whistle and low rumble of a freight train passing by late at night, transporting boxcars of the fruit to destinations far and wide.

That romantic sound has been replaced by the air horns of commuter trains, but at one time the railroads were the lifeline of farmers and ranchers selling their products to the world-at-large.

The coming of the railroad to Orange County wasn't an easy task, however. It was a classic 19th-century power struggle between a seemingly omnipotent railroad company and a stubborn ranch family.

The Southern Pacific Railroad was the first line to enter the farm fields and towns that would become Orange County. It arrived in Anaheim in 1874, linking the area to Los Angeles, San Francisco and the recently completed transcontinental railroad, allowing farmers to sell their oranges, walnuts and other produce to markets around the country.

Collis P. Huntington, founder of the Southern Pacific, had great hopes of extending the line to San Diego along a coastal route through part of the 110,000-acre Irvine Ranch. However, James Irvine, Sr., owner of the ranch that stretched from the Santa Ana Mountains to the ocean, refused to allow the tracks on his land.

According to legend, Irvine's feud with the Southern Pacific began in 1849 when he met Huntington on a Gold Rush steamship from the East Coast. Both were young men looking to make their way in the world.

The two apparently took an intense dislike to each other on the voyage after a disputed poker game. Irvine felt Huntington had cheated in winning a small sum, and remembered it the rest of his life. Incredibly, the two would meet once again as middle-aged men — one a successful cattle rancher, the other heading a powerful railroad company.

When Irvine refused to negotiate whatsoever with Southern Pacific, Huntington sued in federal court saying part of the ranch's boundaries were still under federal domain.

Although a court ruling in 1856 had upheld the boundaries, the Southern Pacific convinced the federal government to reopen the case in 1876. A ruling in his favor would give Huntington large chunks of coastal land on each side of the tracks for development.

Despite Huntington's influence in Washington, the case was decided in favor of the Irvines in 1878 and the ranch remained intact. It was one of the few times when the political power of a railroad company did not win the day in the 1800s.

A little more than a decade later the Atchison, Topeka & Santa Fe arrived in Santa Ana from Riverside and was threatening to take much of Southern Pacific's business from its Orange County line.

Before the Santa Fe's arrival, the Southern Pacific was reportedly taking advantage of its railroad monopoly and price-gouging its customers in Orange County. Many county residents protested the high rates, calling the railroad monolopy "the Octopus" with its "cold, steely tentacles."

A rate war ensued that brought hordes of visitors and prospective home-buyers to the county. Southern Pacific saw the area growing and wanted to move fast to secure the line to San Diego as the county's population boomed.

The Irvine family continued to refuse to negotiate with the company. Using a bullying tactic common to railroad companies of the era, Southern Pacific planned to simply lay tracks on the Irvine land without the ranch family's permission.

The rail workers started from the line's end in Tustin to the edge of the Irvine property one weekend in 1888. They planned to lay as much track as possible across Irvine property while the courts were closed.

Huntington and the Southern Pacific, however, underestimated the moxie of the Irvine ranch hands.

At the edge of the ranch, the track gang was met by angry, gun-toting ranch workers who threatened to open fire if any track crossed Irvine property. They never had to use their guns — the track layers quickly abandoned their chore.

On the following Monday the Irvines obtained a court order blocking any encroachment on their ranch. The tracks which led to nowhere remained in place until 1910.

As a result of the confrontation, the Irvines quickly struck a deal with the Santa Fe. For $4,500 and the right to build roads over the railroad at the Irvines' discretion, Santa Fe got its right of way to construct a line to San Diego. The line was completed in 1889 and still carries Amtrak commuter trains through Orange County to this day.

The Southern Pacific never did gets its railroad through Irvine land. It eventually reached San Diego, winding through Colton, Beaumont and Yuma, Ariz., finally crossing into the city via El Centro — and that didn't happen until the 1930s.

Engineers for the Southern Pacific line at the Tustin station, circa 1900

STORY OF THE COUNTY'S MOST FAMOUS FARM

On a dusty dirt road in 1920, a Buena Park farmer named Walter Knott began selling berries to motorists on their way to the ocean.

It was a humble beginning for what would become one of Southern California's premiere attractions — Knott's Berry Farm. Today the world-famous amusement park stands on the exact site of Knott's original farm and roadside stand.

Success for the Knott family didn't happen overnight. On several occasions they almost lost their small farm. But with a pioneer spirit of determination and hard work, the family persevered.

Knott was originally a sharecropper on a San Luis Obispo farm with his wife Cordelia and their three small children. When his cousin in Orange County offered him a partnership to raise berries on a leased 20-acre farm, Knott agreed and moved his family to their new home in Buena Park.

It was not an easy time. Most of the family's savings went to purchase farming equipment and berry plants, and several heavy frosts nearly wiped them out that first year. Probably the only thing that saved the farm was Walter's business sense.

Knott believed that he could get a better price for his berries if he marketed them himself. So he put up a roadside stand and sold most of his berry crop to the crowds of summer vacationers who drove past the farm on Grand Avenue, now known as Beach Boulevard, on their way to Anaheim Landing, now known as Seal Beach.

To set himself apart, Walter searched for a unique berry that people would prize for their tables. He read a newspaper article about a new hybrid called a "youngberry." He filled a half-acre with the new plants and advertised them to the public and to other grow- ers, eventually grossing more than $2,000 from his investment.

In 1927 an oil boom drove land prices sky high and the farm's owner wanted to sell the property. While his cousin decided to move, Walter couldn't see the point in walking away from a growing concern. He decided to purchase 10 acres at $1,500 an acre.

Now that the property was his, Knott wanted to build a bigger berry stand and a new home for the family. Cordelia told him to "make a big kitchen" because she planned to start canning berries and jam and baking pies for customers.

With Cordelia's help, ever-increasing crowds began showing up, and the business grew until the stock market crash of 1929. Suddenly it cost more to produce the fruit than the price the family could get for it.

Friends urged the Knotts to abandon the high-priced land. But the family decided to stay until the berry farm succeeded or foreclosure took it from them.

Success finally came from Walter's reputation as a berry expert. In 1930 George Darrow, a representative of the U.S. Department of Agriculture, came to him for help.

It seems the USDA had heard of a new berry developed by a Mr. Boysen of Orange County. Did he know anything about it?

Knott had never heard of Mr. Boysen's berry, but when he learned it was a cross between a blackberry, a raspberry and a loganberry, and was larger and more delicious than all three, he became quite interested.

Rudolph Boysen of Anaheim had experimented with the berry several years before, but only six half-dead plants were left in an orange grove. Knott tended the plants carefully until he could move them to his farm. There they grew larger and healthier than all his other berry plants.

The newly named "boysenberry" was the superior berry Knott had been searching for. From its introduction, the boysenberry was in demand for canning, cooking and table eating. In the middle of the Great Depression, Knott's berry farm had all the business it could handle.

As the family's tea room was getting jammed with motorists being served boysenberry pie and biscuits, Cordelia asked her husband to purchase some chickens and cherry rhubarb. The next day, she brought out her wedding china and served eight people chicken dinners and rhubarb appetizers for 65 cents.

Within weeks, a line of people waited outside the tea room at every meal. The Knotts doubled the size of the room, and the crowds kept getting larger. By August of '34 they were serving 85 chicken dinners a day. In 1936, they added more rooms and changed the name of the tea room to the Chicken Dinner Restaurant.

Still the lines grew. Walter Knott wanted a way to entertain the patrons while they waited. He loved Western lore and decided to set up his own Wild West town, dismantling and bringing in actual buildings from an abandoned gold-mining town in Arizona.

First came a hotel, then a saloon, a jail, a schoolhouse, blacksmith's shop and additional shacks. Covered wagons, stage coaches, a Boot Hill cemetery and employees dressed in authentic attire completed the effect.

He didn't know it at the time, but the successful berry farmer had just planted the seeds of the world's first theme park.

The rest, as they say, is history.

Walter and Cordelia Knott's original berry stand

How Horse Racing Came to Orange County

In northern Orange County lies a racetrack that draws thousands of people every week who come to see some real "horse power."

It's the Los Alamitos Race Course, or "Los Al" to track regulars. Located at the county's border, it opened in 1947 and was the first track in California to hold state-sanctioned quarter-horse racing.

First bred by the American Colonists, quarter horses were so-named because farmers discovered they would run for about a quarter mile and stop. Although heavier than the thoroughbreds that run at Santa Anita Race Track, the horses are faster in short-distance races.

The Los Alamitos Race Course was started by entrepreneur Frank Vessels. Vessels was a young man living in the heart of horse country, Kentucky, when he learned about an oil strike in Signal Hill, Calif. The news inspired him to move to Southern California in 1920 with $19 and a change of clothes.

Discovering that wildcatting was an unpredictable business, Vessels started a construction company that built drilling platforms and sold boilers to the oilmen. He struck it rich and went broke four different times along the way. When prosperity finally seemed assured, he was struck by another financially risky idea.

Vessels had purchased a 600-acre farm in Orange County to raise cattle. Like many of his neighbors, Vessels enjoyed watching informal match horse races held throughout the county on Sundays.

Most of the races were all-out sprints and the best horses for that type of racing were quarter horses. Vessels was thrilled with the sheer speed of these equine athletes, and was reminded of the many fine horses from his native state.

Vessels discovered his land was unsuitable for raising cattle, so he hitched a plow to his tractor and etched out an oval in the alkaline soil. He then invited his match-racing friends to bring their horses to his place on Sunday.

On Aug. 3, 1947, more than a thousand people showed up at the inaugural race day. The purse for each race was dictated by the number of entries and ranged between $50 and $100. Although Vessels could not take any bets, many "greenbacks" changed hands among the crowd.

Through 1950 the Sunday races continued to draw crowds. With the track located virtually in Vessels' backyard, his wife Grace would sell "red hots with plenty of mustard" from her kitchen window.

After mounting a campaign with other California breeders, Vessels won the right in 1951 to hold an 11-day, all quarter-horse meet with pari-mutuel wagering. Pari-mutuel is the betting system in which winners share the total stakes, minus a percentage for management.

Although rain fell every day of the meet, more than 30,000 people attended the event, wagering more than $1.5 million. Because the track was left a muddy pool, the Vessels actually lost money at the meet.

With the assistance of his friend Huntley Gordon (great-grandfather of Orange County auto racer Robby Gordon), Frank sank another $100,000 into physical improvements and convinced the California Racing Board to grant the track 16 days of racing the following year.

Business nearly doubled in the 1952 season, proving to everyone that quarter-horse racing was a viable entry into the Southern California sports and entertainment scene.

In 1955, after a modern grandstand was added to the site, a two-year-old named Go Man Go became the track's first superstar. The horse began the first of an unprecedented three consecutive World Championship seasons at Los Alamitos.

He would later prove his dominance at every other track he raced, capturing the imagination of sportswriters and fans who had never before paid attention to quarter-horse racing. As his fame grew, so did the crowds at Los Alamitos, who would chant "Go Man Go" before his every race.

The horse's success spawned the growth in the breeding and racing of quarter horses on a national level. An American Quarter Horse Association was formed, with Vessels as president. Go Man Go became a cornerstone of the breed, and a majority of horses currently racing at Los Alamitos carry his blood.

After his father's death in 1963, Frank Vessels, Jr. helped continue his dad's vision. In 1968 Frank Jr. led Los Alamitos into the realm of night racing, and in 1972 harness racing made its debut. Gate receipts and betting increased every year.

Following the untimely death of Frank Jr., his wife Millie Vessels assumed control of the track. She had been there at the track's infancy, hauling garbage and selling sandwiches, and proved to be a talented businesswoman.

Under Millie's tenure, Los Alamitos became the site of California's first million-dollar horse race. In a period of incredible growth, the track and quarter-horse racing finally grabbed its share of the national spotlight.

In 1981 Millie, wishing to concentrate more on breeding quarter horses, sold the track to Hollywood Park. The owners of Hollywood Park were not well-versed in quarter-horse racing, however, and Los Alamitos started to lose money for the first time.

It was during these stormy years when Ed Allred stepped in to purchase the track. Allred was an Orange County physician who had been a frequent visitor to the track since his medical student days and had a sincere love of its quarter-horse tradition.

In 1990 he purchased one-half interest, and later become majority owner. He mended fences with the other investors and built the Vessels Club inside the clubhouse to honor the track's past, and put the grandson of Frank Vessels, 'Scoop' Vessels, on the board of directors.

Allred is credited with bringing Los Alamitos Race Course back to its former glory.

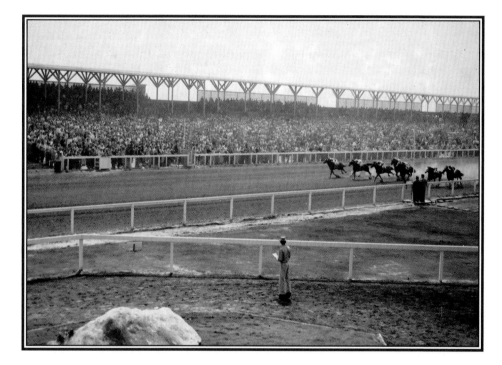

Crowds at Los Alamitos Race Course cheer on Go Man Go in 1955.

HELENA MODJESKA - THE FIRST STAR OF THE COUNTY

Celebrities have been calling Orange County home for years, from John Wayne and Harriet Nelson to Buddy Ebsen and Jose Felicíano.

But perhaps the first celebrity to ever live here was an actress named Helena Modjeska, who made her home in the foothills of the Santa Ana Mountains during the 1880s and 90s.

She was one of the most popular actresses of her day, performing with Maurice Barrymore (patriarch of the acting family) and Edwin Booth, brother of Lincoln's assassin and the best-known actor of the time.

I recently visited her restored home in what is now Modjeska Canyon and met with historian Ellen Lee who told me the details of the actress' life.

Born in Poland, Modjeska was a legendary actress in her homeland by the 1870s. She performed in the Warsaw Theater, which was overseen by the Russian czarist government.

Apparently, Modjeska didn't like the censorship of her plays by theater officials. She also dreamed of an American theatrical career that other European actresses had successfully started.

So in 1876 Modjeska and her husband, Count Karol Bozenta Chlapowski, moved to the U.S. with a small group of friends. They chose to settle in Anaheim after hearing about ranch land for sale at cheap prices.

The couple purchased a 20-acre vineyard. The Count went to work on the small ranch while Modjeska took a train to San Francisco to start an acting career in this country.

She first had to relearn her Shakespearean roles in English. At age 36, she taught herself to speak English well enough to make her debut on stages in San Francisco and New York just a year after her arrival.

She later spent time in England taking additional speech lessons to hide her Polish accent. Upon her return to the U.S. she became a celebrated actress, touring in a private rail car and playing theaters, halls and opera houses throughout the country.

Though their Anaheim vineyard had failed, Modjeska and Count Bazenta returned to Orange County in 1884 to visit friend Joseph Pleasants on his Santiago Canyon ranch.

The couple fell in love with the canyon area and bought part interest in the Pleasants' ranch. In 1888 they purchased the remaining ranch with plans to remodel a simple existing cabin.

Modjeska enlisted famed New York architect Stanford White to draw plans for the additions to the cabin. Working from photographs and sketches, White designed an elaborate five-gabled manor against the backdrop of hills and live oak trees.

The house and grounds appear today much as they did in Modjeska's time. In front of the house are two fountains, a wishing well, palm trees, and spacious lawns with rose gardens and flower beds. Nearby is a large swimming pool.

She called the estate "Forest of Arden" after the fictional forest in Shakespeare's "As You Like It."

Arden became well-known for its rustic beauty and the hospitality of its owners. County pioneers were regular visitors, including the Rice family of Tustin, the Langenbergers of Anaheim and the Yochs of Santa Ana.

Most visitors took the train to an El Toro depot where a horse and buggy would be waiting for their 10-mile journey to Arden. After the long trip, many would stay a few days to relax and enjoy the natural setting.

In those days before movies or TV, actors would travel most of the year. So for Modjeska, Arden was a peaceful retreat where she rested, prepared costumes for the next tour and studied her roles.

It was said she would walk the grounds of Arden rehearsing her lines for her next play. It was an image her fans liked to have of her.

Modjeska was a permanent fixture at benefits and society dinners in Orange County. In 1892 she opened the Santa Ana Opera House in a benefit performance for a local orphanage. She also played the piano or acted small scenes from plays at parties for her county friends.

In addition to being an artist's hideaway, Arden was also a 1,300-acre working ranch and olive farm. But the ranch never made money and in 1904 the couple sold the property.

For a time they rented a house in Tustin, then moved to a beach cottage on Bay Island in Newport Beach. It was there Modjeska died on April 8, 1909.

After her death, Count Bazenta placed a plaque on the grounds of Arden where Modjeska often sat memorizing lines beneath an oak tree.

She is buried with her husband in Poland where she is considered the country's greatest actress of all time. The city theater in her native Krakow is named for her.

Here in Orange County a statue of Modjeska can be found in Pearson Park in Anaheim. It was constructed during the '30s as part of a public works project. It shows her in costume from her favorite role as Mary, Queen of Scots.

Helena Modjeska's 'Forest of Arden' in the foothills of the Santa Ana mountains.

Cook's Corner, OC's Wild West Roadhouse

If you had to name one classic "dive" in Orange County for posterity, it would have to be Cook's Corner in the foothills of the Santa Ana Mountains.

While the rest of the county has been overrun with mainstream restaurant chains and bars, Cook's prides itself on being unconventional, untamed and uncivilized like many of the canyon residents who live nearby.

The bar and burger joint sits on the northeast corner of a Y-shaped intersection joining Santiago Canyon, Live Oak Canyon and El Toro roads. On the opposite corner lies the entrance to St. Michael's Seminary, making it a crossroads of sorts for sinners and saints.

A converted World War II Army mess hall, visitors are greeted with a sign on the door that says "No Firearms," and a sawdust-covered dance floor awaits the "prettiest country girls you ever saw" (according to the Cook's Corner menu) who come to dance to country-western bands on the weekends.

Many of Cook's modern-day patrons arrive on horseback, while others line the front with their motorcycles. Both groups are often in boots and other Western gear.

During its 70-year history, Cook's clientele has included poachers and Polish royalty, cowboys and miners. As Orange County historian Jim Sleeper once said, "A great many prominent countians have visited Cook's Corner over the years, but many would never acknowledge it."

Cook's Corner traces its beginnings to the late 1800s when the mountain area was settled by Southern homesteaders looking for a new start and some cheap land. Most were beekeepers, wood choppers, miners and goat herders.

The settler to originally stake out the corner was Andrew Frame, who took up the land in 1870. In 1881 he sold the land to Joseph Dameron, who traded the property with its adjoining 190 acres to Andrew Cook in 1883 for land on Palomar Mountain.

Little was done to develop the property at first. In 1886 the Aliso School District held its first classes at the future site of the roadhouse. Nineteen students with 10 books sat under sycamore trees daily until a schoolhouse was finished half-a-mile up the road.

It wasn't until 1926 that Earl Jack (E. J.) Cook, son of Andrew, opened a tiny hamburger joint at the corner with his wife Irene. The operation was a sidelight to their modest hog and cattle ranch.

A converted beekeepers' cabin, the place had room for only six stools. Old-timers have said it didn't become a popular hangout until the repeal of Prohibition in 1933. Once the beer began to flow, Cook's Corner became a favorite stop for canyon residents.

Conversation at the roadhouse typically revolved around the weather, bears, mines, hunting and the latest character to secure a place in the hills.

In the early days much was made about Count Bozenta, the husband of famed Polish actress and canyon resident Madame Modjeska, who would ride his bicycle to the corner and pick up mail, dressed in his fine silk shirts and smoking his hand-rolled cigarettes.

Other canyon eccentrics to stop by included semi-hermit Holy Jim Smith, Jake Yeager, the county's most consistently optimistic miner, and Uncle Jimmy Shaw, a local chicken rancher who would entertain patrons with his fiddle-playing.

In 1946 E.J. Cook dismantled a mess hall from the Santa Ana Army Air Base and reassembled it across the street from the original establishment. The long, low military barracks consisted mostly of strips of asphalt tacked on wooden boards. It may not have won any architectural awards, but it offered more room for Cook's clientele and the price was right — it cost nothing.

E.J. died in 1960, and his wife Irene ran the business until 1963 when she began leasing the establishment. It was during this time Cook's gained its reputation as a biker bar, becoming a favorite stop for guys on hogs with their tattooed girlfriends.

Cook's employees had to be as tough as their clientele, and included a 230-pound cook named "Twiggy" and a woman bartender who reportedly killed the last mountain lion in Trabuco Canyon.

In 1976 Volker Stricek, owner of a motorcycle accessories shop in Santa Ana, purchased Cook's Corner with partner Victor Villa. Many of the original motorcyclists continued to stop by through the 1980s, though now they had become businessmen and were raising families.

While other county landmarks have fallen by the wayside, Cook's has somehow resisted the pressures of development thus far, seeming to have an untouchable aura.

In the late '80s, it was almost demolished to widen El Toro Road for the increasing traffic, but the plan was nixed. Later, a developer's plan to build a 50,000-square-foot shopping center also fell by the wayside.

Cook's present owner Frank de Luna wants to develop the corner, too, but says he will keep the roadside establishment and build a 19,000-square-foot retail mall behind it. He also plans to erect a 222-acre subdivision across the street.

For the time being, Cook's Corner remains the same. On any given afternoon, you can still hear the strains of bluegrass music, the clinking of beer bottles and patrons' discussions about their Harleys gleaming in the sun.

Cook's Corner, a favorite county watering hole for 70 years

MODERN-DAY ORANGE COUNTY BORN AT SANTA ANA AIR BASE

Looking at Orange County's sprawling development today, it's hard to imagine that prior to World War II, it was mostly a farming community of just 130,000 people.

Most local historians agree that what sparked the county's dramatic growth, and changed the area forever, started in October 1941.

That was the month ground broke at the site of the Santa Ana Army Air Base, an aviation cadet classification center and pre-flight training school run during World War II. Soon 150,000 men and women poured onto the base from all around the country.

Most would probably never have ventured that far from home if the war had not taken place. But those who were stationed at the base liked what they saw in Orange County: an idyllic climate, picturesque beaches and a rural lifestyle.

"When the war was over, many would return to escape the two 'S's back home — swatting mosquitoes in the summer and shoveling snow in the winter," said base historian Bud Anderson of Huntington Beach.

By 1950 the population of the county increased to 216,000. The next twenty years saw it skyrocket to 1.4 million, and today the population stands at 2.6 million. A dramatic change had taken place as a result of World War II.

Anderson, a former cadet at the base, said the Santa Ana Army Air Base was one of three bases President Roosevelt put into action in anticipation of America's involvement in the war. Of the three, the Santa Ana base was the largest, with more than 800 buildings on 1,300 acres of land.

Despite its name, the base never featured a landing strip or a single plane and was located in what is now Costa Mesa, not Santa Ana. The main purpose of the base was to test and assign servicemen as pilots, bombardiers or navigators. The cadets would go on to flight schools in California and Arizona.

The massive classification center was located between Harbor and Newport boulevards on what was then county land, covering what is now Orange Coast College, Southern California College, Costa Mesa High School and the Orange County Fairgrounds. The base received its name because the headquarters were located on Eighth and Flower in Santa Ana.

Anderson said the Santa Ana Army Air Base was a beehive of activity during the war years, where young men trained intensively from 5 a.m. until 9 p.m. every day for two months.

"All the classes were accelerated," Anderson explained. "We had 'two plus two' through calculus in about 50 days.

"We took physics, algebra, maps and charts, aerial navigation, aircraft recognition. It was often said by cadets that if you dropped your pencil you'd miss two years of regular college instruction."

In addition to accelerated classes, the cadets underwent vigorous physical and mental conditioning, including spending time in a pressurized room that simulated high-altitude conditions. About 24,000 of the cadets "washed out" and were re-assigned to other aircraft-related duties.

"We would also practice shooting 'tommy guns' from Huntington Beach at targets in the ocean," Anderson recalled. "There must be a ton of lead out there (on the ocean floor)."

Because of its close proximity to Hollywood, the air base was the site of national radio broadcasts starring Bob Hope, Jack Benny, Eddie Cantor, Alan Ladd and Edgar Bergen. Many celebrities also went through the cadet program, such as Jimmy Stewart, Gene Autry and Tom Harmon, or worked on the base, like baseball legend Joe DiMaggio, who was a physical education instructor.

After six weeks at the base, the servicemen received a weekend pass, and restaurants and bars throughout Orange County were mobbed. Popular nightspots included the Rendezvous Ballroom in Balboa, the Palm Palm Drive-in and Cafe and the Cadet Cafe in Costa Mesa, the Stag Cafe in Newport Beach, and the Pav-a-lon in Huntington Beach.

"The base was an incredible lift to the economy of Orange County," Anderson said. "With it came the addition of hundreds of new jobs."

Toward the war's end, the base was used in the rehabilitation of men returning from German and Japanese prisoner-of-war camps. It also served as a redistribution center for 78,000 air force combat veterans. The gates of the Santa Ana Army Air Base were closed on March 31, 1946.

Only a few of the base buildings remain at the Orange County Fairgrounds and at Orange Coast College. But the air base's legacy lives on.

For years after the war, men and women who had been stationed there would tell relatives and friends of a beautiful oceanside community in Southern California.

Paradise had been found.

Santa Ana Army Air Base, a WWII training center

THE O'NEILLS - COUNTY'S PIONEER RANCH FAMILY

During family outings through south Orange County years ago, we would see nothing but endless hills of sagebrush and grazing cattle.

What I didn't know at the time is that we were passing through the O'Neill family ranch, one of the largest of the old Spanish ranchos and the last to be developed in the county.

The O'Neills and the ranch have a storied history that stretches from Ireland of the 1800s, to the California Gold Rush, to World War II and beyond.

Born in County Cork in 1825, as a child Richard O'Neill moved with his parents to flee the grinding poverty of Ireland during the 1830s.

The family settled in Boston, where Richard apprenticed as a butcher under his father's tutelage. But the young man had bigger dreams. After hearing of the gold strike in 1849, Richard caught the next ship to California.

Along the way he met fellow Irishman James Flood and the two became friends. When they discovered gold wasn't as plentiful as they imagined, they started businesses next door to each other in San Francisco.

Flood opened a bar and exchange where miners could trade their gold for cash, while O'Neill opened a butcher shop. Both men prospered, but Flood was the most successful. A few years after starting the tavern, Flood became co-owner of the famed Comstock Lode in Nevada and a founder of Wells Fargo Bank.

O'Neill, whose business grew by selling meat to the Army and to merchant ships, wanted to start a cattle business. By the 1880s, he was looking for range land to start his own ranch.

In 1882 he learned that longtime rancher Don Juan Forster of San Juan Capistrano had died. Forster owned a 233,000-acre ranch called the Santa Margarita that stretched from present-day Lake Forest to Oceanside.

Because of a severe drought, the ranch was in a bad financial state and Forster's three sons were interested in selling the land. O'Neill went to his old friend James Flood and on a handshake the two agreed to purchase the ranch.

Flood provided $250,000 in gold to buy the property, but both men held equal shares. The pair decided to have O'Neill manage the ranch and repay his half from future profits.

When O'Neill arrived in Orange County, he discovered the ranch in disrepair and poorly stocked with cattle. The butcher-turned-rancher brought in Texas shorthorns, irrigated the land to raise feed crops and hired more vaqueros.

In a short time, he had made the ranch a success and won the respect of many in the business as a shrewd and efficient cattleman.

When O'Neill was past 80 and broken in health, James Flood, Jr. made good on his father's promise and deeded half of the ranch to the patriarch. The elderly man passed the torch to his son Jerome, who furthered the success of the ranch.

Upon Richard O'Neill's death, Jerome inherited the half interest. Wanting to keep the ranch intact as their fathers' wished, Flood and O'Neill formed the Rancho Santa Margarita Corp. in the 1920s so the ranch would not be sold after their deaths.

Upon Jerome's death in 1926, equal shares of his stock were left to his sister, Mary Baumgartner, and his brother, Richard. However, the stock was held in a trust and the ranch's fortunes began to decline under conservative control of trust officers.

In 1940 the ranch was divided between all the heirs — the Floods retained the southernmost section in San Diego County, while the Baumgartners held the northern section of San Diego County. Richard O'Neill, Jr. was given the Orange County holdings.

During World War II, the Marine Corps commandeered the two San Diego County parcels to build the Camp Pendleton training base. The Floods were happy to sell their parcel, but the Baumgartners unsuccessfully tried to retrieve the land after the war.

The O'Neills were left with the only remaining ranch land. Marguerite "Daisy" O'Neill took charge of operations following her husband Richard's death in 1943. She fought to keep the bank from selling the property several times and kept the ranch intact. Marguerite lived to be 102 and is still considered the family heroine.

Through the 1950s, the O'Neills had strained relations with the trust officers, who never invested money to make improvements at the ranch. But the land values soared as the county slowly developed. The per acre price rose from $800 to $5,000 during the decade.

It wasn't until 1963 the O'Neills made their first foray into selling parcels for development. They sold 80 percent interest in 10,000 acres to Donald Bren, who would later purchase The Irvine Company and build Mission Viejo.

During the '70s, Anthony Moiso, the great-grandson of Richard O'Neill, convinced the family they should develop the land themselves rather than sell it off piecemeal. Moiso believed the family could better control the quality of the developments and keep more of the profits.

Through loans, Moiso acquired a $56-million parcel from the estate and formed the Santa Margarita Company. He began work on the community of Rancho Santa Margarita in the mid-80s, considered an innovative development today.

Even with development, large tracts of pristine land remain on the O'Neill ranch. There is still a working cattle business, the largest in Southern California, and every year there is a festive round-up party for the spring branding.

That's a touch family patriarch and cattleman Richard O'Neill probably would have appreciated.

The O'Neill ranch, the last Spanish rancho to be developed in Orange County

When Pirates Attacked the Capistrano Mission

When people consider the history of Mission San Juan Capistrano, most think of Spanish padres, Native Americans and returning swallows.

An interesting footnote to its history, though, is that the mission was once sacked by a famous pirate.

The pirate's name was Hippolyte Bouchard, a Frenchman who fought against the English in the Napoleonic wars. By the time he was just 20 he had captained his first ship, a frigate named the Argentine, assisting revolutionaries in Buenos Aires attempting to overthrow Spanish rule in the New World.

He continued fighting in various actions against the Spanish Armada, then began a career sacking all seafaring vessels and port cities around the world. In 1816 he sailed to Hawaii and reclaimed an Argentine ship called the Santa Rosa.

Bouchard now had two pirate ships under his command with roughly 350 of the worst scoundrels on the high seas from California, the Philippines, Malaysia, Portugal and Argentina. The privateers also had 50 stolen muskets and a half-dozen cannons on board.

On Oct. 20, 1818, the ship set sail from Hawaii headed for Monterey, the political center of Spanish California. Warned of the pirates' course, Spanish settlements all along the coast moved their valuables inland.

Bouchard and his men sacked and burned Monterey for five days. As a force of 200 Spanish soldiers gathered to retake the demolished city, Bouchard weighed anchor.

Next, he and his men raided a seaside rancho north of Santa Barbara. They then set sail for San Juan Capistrano, the last chance to get provisions before sailing home to South America.

On Dec. 14, 1818 the two pirate ships sailed into what is now Dana Point Harbor in an early morning fog. As the fog lifted, Bouchard could see the Capistrano Mission high on a hill, its white stucco facade in sharp contrast to the brown hillsides of the future Orange County.

An English pirate aboard named Peter Corney wrote in his journal:

"We ran into a snug bay in latitude 33 degrees, 33 minutes north, where we anchored under a flag of truce. The bay is well-sheltered, with a most beautiful town and mission, about two leagues from the beach."

Just 32 years earlier, Father Junipero Serra had established the mission near the harbor midway between Mission San Diego and the pueblo of Los Angeles.

Unlike other missions founded in California, San Juan Capistrano had been successful from the start, with good water, productive vineyards and a profitable hide-tanning trade. It was known as "la jolla" or "the jewel" of the missions. Because of its success, rumors of treasures abounded, with many believing there were gold coins and gems hidden by the padres on the mission property.

Whatever the mission had in treasures, Bouchard still had to land and get gunpowder, water and supplies. And San Diego had to be avoided at all costs because it was heavily fortified and waiting for him.

A messenger was sent from Bouchard under a flag of truce demanding the mission town provide the needed supplies. The pirate was usually able to intimidate townspeople into complying with his demands.

What Bouchard didn't know was that a garrison of some 30 men had been dispatched by Commandant Ruize of San Diego after being notified of two pirate ships sailing down the coast.

Alferez Arguello was the leader of the small Spanish force posted on a hill near the mission. He sent the messenger back with surprising news. Bouchard's demands had been turned down flat with a promise that if the pirates didn't shove off, they would be met with "an immediate supply of shot and shell."

Bouchard was enraged. He ordered a landing of 70 men and three cannons to attack the town and the mission, stripping it of provisions and treasures.

The advance up the hill was slow and difficult. The cannons' wheels buried themselves in the dry soil. Six pirates were hurt, though not killed, by a few scattered shots. It was a later scandal that the soldiers fled with the residents to the hills above the town. They stood and watched as the invaders sacked one house after another.

A shout was heard as the wine storage was discovered on the mission grounds. The pirates began a revelry that lasted all day. Private homes, stores and barracks were set afire by Bouchard and his men.

Corney wrote, "We found the town well-stocked with everything but money, and destroyed much wine and spirits and all the public property. At about two o'clock, we marched back, though not in the order we went, many of the men being intoxicated."

About 20 men were so drunk they had to be lashed to cannons and dragged back down the beach. The carriage of one cannon fell apart and was abandoned near the mission.

Four men slipped away in the confusion and deserted the pirate crew, including: Mateo Jose Pascual, considered to be the first black person ever to set foot on county soil; John Rose, a drummer in the Scottish army; and two natives of Buenos Aires. Two women from San Juan Capistrano joined the pirates.

After taking all the available food and supplies, Bouchard decided it was time to leave San Juan. Four days after the attack, when his crew was sober again, the Argentine and the Santa Rosa sailed away with the tide.

Bouchard's timing couldn't have been better. A well-armed militia of Native Americans, led by Father Luis Martinez of Santa Barbara, had followed the two ships after their northern raid and marched into Capistrano the day after Bouchard set sail.

No treasures were ever discovered by the pirates. And the inhabitants of Mission San Juan Capistrano were able to rebound from their meeting with the baddest man of the high seas.

For his daring exploits against the Spanish Armada, Bouchard was rewarded with an officer's position in the Peruvian Navy. The former pirate had become respectable.

Mission San Juan Capistrano was sacked by pirate Hippolyte Bouchard in 1818.

HERALDING THE NEW YEAR ON BALBOA ISLAND FERRY

One of the best New Year's Eves I ever spent wasn't at a party packed with people. It was with a date gliding through the waters of Newport Harbor on the Balboa Island Ferry.

We had plans to meet friends at a restaurant on the Newport peninsula, but car trouble had us running very late. We decided to take the short-cut across the water when midnight struck.

With the sounds of revelers far off in the distance, she and I were alone on the ferry boat entranced by the quiet and the lights of the Fun Zone reflecting on the water. Not a bad way to begin the New Year.

Many New Years later, I still look back on that evening and think of that scenic ride across the bay. This year I decided to visit the offices of the Balboa Island Ferry Company to find out more about this 75-year-old Orange County institution.

According to Marcia Swanson of the ferry's office, an amazing 2.5-million locals and tourists from around the world cross the waters of the harbor every year on the ferries. With so many people crossing, the ferry pilots have seen it all, she said.

"We've had several weddings and many engagements on the boats," Swanson said. "Six years ago a limousine got on board and a couple got married before they reached the other side. The joke among the pilots was they got divorced before they returned."

Celebrities who have resided in the area were often ferry regulars, including John Wayne, Buddy Ebsen and Joey Bishop. In recent years "Melrose Place" star Heather Locklear rode the ferry daily. Then there was the Elvis impersonator.

"He was this funny guy who used to walk around with his hair slicked back and a boom box playing Elvis songs," Swanson said. "I think he really thought he was the King, and some of the pilots thought so after awhile."

Five cars and one motorcycle have accidentally driven off the boats in past years. People used to jump off the ferry as part of birthday celebrations, she said, but don't anymore since the bay has gotten "murkier."

Through the years passengers have sometimes fished during the ride, although it is forbidden today. Sharks, eels and rays have all been pulled aboard.

The ferry has remained in operation for all this time not just because it's a pleasant ride. It also remains the quickest way to travel between Balboa Island and the Newport Beach peninsula.

The only other route to the Newport Beach peninsula is Pacific Coast Highway, which can take a good 15 minutes. For pedestrians, it would be quicker to swim.

Why hasn't the ferry been replaced by a bridge?

"They can't build a bridge," said ferry pilot Lenny Andersen. "Some of the boats in the harbor are more than 150-feet high and you can't build a bridge with that high a clearance over 150 yards of water."

The ferry service first opened in 1909 with "Captain" John Watts at the helm. The Captain was known to sing as he shuttled passengers in a large row boat named the Teal. He was said to regard the bay waters as his private domain, loudly voicing his disapproval whenever other boats came too close.

After changing owners several times following Watts, the City of Newport Beach awarded a contract to Balboa Island resident Joseph Beek in 1919 to operate the ferry. Beek's three sons Seymour, Allan and Barton still operate the service to this day.

Beek, who later became a state legislator and prominent real estate developer, started his ferry business in an oversized row boat called the Ark. Though it was equipped with an outboard motor, the pair of oars often came in handy whenever the cantankerous motor would stop working.

He added a larger boat in 1920 known as the Fat Ferry which was in service for more than 20 years. The next year a small barge was lashed to the bow of the Fat Ferry for transporting automobiles. The ferry would push the barge with a car across the water. It must have been a treacherous endeavor, but it worked.

The first self-propelled auto ferry went into service the next year. Named the Joker, it carried two cars and had a propeller at each end so they didn't have to turn around with each crossing. In 1930 the first three-car ferry called the Commodore was added to the fleet.

That same year the Balboa Island Ferry was granted a certificate to operate by the Public Utility Commission of the state of California, making it the smallest public utility in the state. It remains so today.

During the 1950s, three new 64-foot diesel-powered boats were built that were safer than the gas engines of the previous ferries and offered more room. The three boats, which are still in operation today, are the Admiral, the Captain and the Commodore.

The boats can carry 100 passengers, including pilot and fare collector, and up to four cars and make as many as eight round trips per hour.

Fares have jumped a little since Joseph Beek charged five cents for the trip across the bay in his rowboat, but the prices are still reasonable. Cost is $1 for car and driver, 60 cents for those on bikes, and 35 cents for pedestrians. Kids 5 to 11 cost 15 cents, while those under 5 ride free.

The ferry does stop operating during violent storms, but usually for just a couple of hours. Otherwise, it's in operation throughout the year, including New Year's Eve.

"It's part of our heritage in Newport Beach," Swanson said. "I'm sure we'll be ferrying cars across 75 years from now."

That should give me a chance to ring in a New Year on the bay again sometime.

Ferry service across Newport Harbor first began in 1909.

DRAG RACING'S ROOTS TRACED TO OC AIRPORT

In the early 1950s, Orange County was a quiet community of orange groves and dairy farms. Who would ever believe that the high-octane world of drag racing would be born in this tranquil setting?

But it was. The first commercial drag races ever held on the planet took place July 2, 1950 on the west runway at the old Orange County Airport in Santa Ana. The airport was located off Main Street near the present site of the John Wayne Airport.

Called "Every Sunday Drag Races," amateur racers from all over Southern California would converge on the quarter-mile track, setting world records and creating new technology that laid the groundwork for today's dragsters.

Admission for both participants and spectators was one of the best deals in motorsports history — a whopping 50 cents.

The weekly races were held until 1959 when the runway was needed for the growing airplane traffic. The events were the brain-child of oil distributor and car enthusiast Creighton Hunter of Santa Ana and his partners C.J. Hart and Frank Stillwell.

"We started the races to get kids off the streets and give them a safe and legal place to race," said Hunter, now retired. "They were popular right from the start."

The hundreds of hot-rodders and motorcyclists who came to the airport raced only for trophies and bragging rights to owning the fastest car or cycle — there were no big money prizes. These were also the days when racers prided themselves on a "do-it-yourself" credo, dialing in their own engines and building creative chassis set-ups.

"We never had lights to start us, didn't even have a clock for quite awhile," Hunter remembered. "It was real simple — whoever got to the finish line first won the race."

Many major names from drag racing's early days cut their teeth at the Orange County Airport runway. Racing promoter Mickey Thompson raced there, as did 'TV' Tommy Ivo, a Hollywood actor. Peggy Hart, the wife of co-promoter C.J. Hart, was one of the first to race there, too, and is likely the first female drag racer ever.

Art Chrisman, who today is a much-admired classic car restorer and hot-rod builder in Santa Ana, often posted the best times of the day in his famous Number 25 car. Like so many other racers, Chrisman started racing in the dry lake beds of the desert.

Chrisman was the first in the nation to reach 140 mph on a dragstrip, setting the record at the airport runway. He has kept the car and restored it, and still brings it to nostalgia racing events.

"I was about 20 when the races began and I went right off the street and the dry lakes and onto the strip," Chrisman said. "It was a friendly competition back then, with everyone helping each other with their cars. Today it costs millions of dollars to compete."

Perhaps the most famous of the cars which appeared at the airport strip was the fabled "Bean Bandit," built and driven by Joaquin Arnette of San Diego. The 1927 T-roadster was equipped with a flat-head Ford engine, and was one of the first to use nitromethane for fuel. During its heyday, the car was practically unbeatable, gaining national notoriety among early drag racing fans and competitors.

The drag races were made possible because of Hunter's friendships with the airport owners, brothers Eddie and Floyd Martin, and Santa Ana mayor Courtney Chandler. Once he got an OK from the city, Hunter promoted the races with flyers stapled on telephone poles and a banner outside the airport. Word of the races spread quickly among hot-rodders.

In the middle of Orange County's farm fields, the racers often posted the fastest times in the country. Top speeds grew quickly from 109 mph in the event's first year to 155 mph by 1955.

To keep the races competitive, the racers were divided between several classes, including roadsters, pre- and post-war stock cars, and motorcycles.

The last race of the day pitted the two racers with the best times, and was often a duel between a motorcycle and hot rod — rarely seen in drag racing anymore. One of the motorcyclists was usually Chet Herbert, owner of Herbert Cams in Anaheim, riding "The Beast."

Hunter himself ran a Mercury-powered roadster with double zeroes as his car's numbers. For fun, he painted the zeroes to look like eyes, which auto parts retailer Dean Moon later made famous as the "Moon Eyes" racing logo.

Hunter later ran a dragster equipped with dolly wheels to raise the car off the ground, get the rear tires spinning, then drop down and blast off in a cloud of smoke and burning rubber.

"It was a time of innovation," Chrisman said. "No two cars were the same. There were dual engines, engines in the front, engines in the back, four-wheel drive — anything that could make you go 1,325 feet quicker than anybody else."

One of the design features that stuck was the long-nosed, "rail" or "slingshot" dragster that is synonymous with top-fuel drag racing today. Cars with the design first appeared at the airport runway.

Both Hunter and Chrisman said they miss the days when Southern California was the dragstrip capital of the country, with tracks in Fontana, Colton, San Diego, Saugus, Irwindale and elsewhere. The list went on and on.

"I'd like to see a track open here again," Chrisman said. "Because this is where it all started."

Fans surround driver Creighton Hunter at the OC airport drag races.

Getting into the Holiday Spirit at Newland House

Every year I think I won't get the holiday spirit, then something happens that brings it to life.

It could be hearing carolers singing, taking home the Christmas tree, or seeing kids gathered around a Santa Claus. This year I found the holiday mood when I viewed the historic Newland House in Huntington Beach.

I was in a shopping center near Beach Boulevard and Adams Avenue when I noticed the house on a hill overlooking the parking lot. Electric candles were lit in the windows and wreaths hung from the doors. It looked like an inviting place to spend some time.

So I went inside, where I met Marsha Johnston, education director for the city's Historical Society.

Johnston told me the house was built by the pioneering Newland family in 1897. It was one of the first ever built in the area, and pre-dates the city itself. It stands at its original location, now restored and open to the public.

As we walked through the rooms there were decorations representing gifts from the traditional song "The Twelve Days of Christmas" that added to the holiday atmosphere.

All the displays, from the twelve drummers drumming to a partridge in a pear tree, looked like decorations from an old-fashioned Christmas 100 years ago. They were designed by the Assistance League of Huntington Beach in conjunction with the Huntington Beach Historical Society.

The Newlands built the 2400-square-foot Victorian-style farmhouse on high flat land above a marsh known as Gospel Swamp. It was in this house the Newlands raised their 10 children — seven girls and three boys.

Originally from Illinois farm country, the Newlands moved to the Los Angeles area in the 1880s, spurred by newspaper stories of rich farmland available at low prices.

Mr. Newland first worked on the Irvine ranch where he gained a reputation as a knowledgeable farmer. When he purchased property on the marshy coast, though, most people thought he had been taken. But he proved them wrong.

Newland drained the water into the ocean and, with the help of neighbors, cut the vegetation and recovered the rich soil for cultivation.

The fertile valley soon became nationally known for producing a variety of quality crops, including celery, lima beans, chili peppers and sugar beets.

For several years the Newland family lived much the way other pioneers did in the 1800s. They carted water into the house with buckets from a water tower out back, and used kerosene lamps to light the house at night.

During the harvest season, the family would hire some 50 extra farmhands to help out. Mrs. Newland would prepare meals daily in the tiny kitchen for everyone on the farm.

The dining room was the most popular place in the house because of a fireplace that provided the only heat source in winter. A "pass-through" opening in the pantry allowed meals to be delivered to the dining table easily.

All the children helped their parents on the farm. The boys would often go on week-long trips to gather and chop firewood, while the girls would cook and tend the chickens.

The Newland farm grew and grew. The family added cows, turkeys, goats and a stock of mules and horses. Other buildings were added, including barns, stables, corrals and bunkhouses.

Surrounding the farmhouse was a vegetable garden, berry bushes and an orchard. Peacocks could be found in the house yard.

In 1915 two of the Newland daughters became ill, so the family added a sun porch to the house. One of the daughters lived in a Palm Springs sanitarium for a time with tuberculosis, and Mrs. Newland would make the two-day horse-and-buggy trip by herself to visit her. Both girls fully recovered.

Mr. Newland's office for a time was a second-story, octagonal tower in front that offered a magnificent view on clear days, ranging from Long Beach to Newport Beach. He found it impractical, though, so it later became a sewing room for his wife.

A nursery was strategically placed adjacent to the parents' room. Mary Newland enjoyed rocking the babies at night with a lullaby and her rocker is still in the room.

The Newlands were not only successful farmers, they were community leaders. They believed strongly in education, and served on the school boards for both the elementary and high schools. Several of their children would later become teachers in Orange County schools.

Mr. Newland also helped finance the city's first bank and the Huntington Beach News, the city's first newspaper. The family were also well-known members of the First Methodist Church.

William Newland died in 1933, but the farm continued under Mary Newland's direction through the 1940s. The family lived in the house until Mary's death in 1952.

I left the Newland House with the impression that these pioneering people placed a high value on family and community. They based their lives around both.

It reminded me this holiday season that even though the world has changed, family and community continue to be what life is all about.

The Victorian farmhouse built by the Newland family, Huntington Beach pioneers

THE ORIGINS OF A GOOD OL' COUNTY FAIR

With all the high-tech entertainment around these days, you may think the simple pleasures of a county fair have lost their appeal.

Nothing could be further from the truth. The Orange County Fair rolled into its 104th year more popular than ever, attracting thousands of local residents who still appreciate the finer points of hog contests, pie bake-offs and petunia competitions.

Last year the fair drew a record 698,000 people and exceeded that number during this year's 16-day event. More than 20,000 entries were submitted from county residents young and old in such categories as floriculture, gems and minerals, livestock and home arts and crafts.

As you might guess, the fair's roots stretch deep into the county's agricultural past.

It began in 1892 as a rivalry between farmers in Los Angeles County and newly incorporated Orange County. Thousands came out to the Santa Ana Racetrack one summer day to see Silkwood, a horse bred in Orange County, race against a three-year-old filly named McKinney, touted by Angelenos as the fastest horse around.

In addition to the main event, there was prize livestock on display and agricultural exhibits at French's Opera House in downtown Santa Ana. Silkwood won the race going away.

As Silkwood continued to win in the ensuing years, the fairgrounds grew also, with a grandstand, stables, livestock exhibit, sheds and corrals. When Silkwood lost his first race in 1895, however, interest in the fair flagged.

The fair reopened in 1897 and rather than focus on horse racing alone, there was a wider variety of events and exhibits, a sumptuous barbecue and the first Ladies Day.

If the first decade of the fair was helped by horsepower, the second owed its success to electricity. With the arrival of the Red Cars of the Pacific Electric Railroad in the fall of 1906, more people attended than ever before.

A "Parade of Products" was featured in the 1906 fair. Horse-drawn floats loaded with the largest and best produce and livestock in the area made their way down Fourth Street in Santa Ana. It was such a popular addition that the fair was renamed the Carnival of Products the next few years.

Prize competitions for farming and homemaking skills were established at this time. Considerable friendly rivalry took place during these contests as people from across the county gathered each year to renew acquaintances and engage in good-natured competition.

The fair was suspended during World War I, but re-emerged in Huntington Beach as the Harvest Home Festival. For two years, exhibits were shown in tents erected on Main Street.

The Santa Ana Chamber of Commerce returned the fair to the city in 1920. Five years later an Orange County Fair Board was established by the local Farm Bureau. The board purchased a 13-acre site across from the Orange County Hospital and the fair was held there until Depression-era conditions halted the event.

In 1937 the fair was revived again, this time with a colorful horse show and rodeo which is still featured today. This incarnation of the fair continued until the start of World War II.

Following the war, the California Department of Agriculture formed the 32nd District Agricultural Association and gave it sole responsibility for putting on the Orange County Fair. The state purchased 175 acres of the former Santa Ana Army Air Base from the Department of Defense as a permanent site for the fairgrounds.

In 1949 the modern-day Orange County Fair was established. Utilizing the abandoned air base buildings, the fair drew an estimated 40,000 attendees.

During the '50s the fair started a tradition of themes. Throughout the decade, the agricultural fair featured a pirate theme, naming a "Pirate Queen" each year. In the '60s, the perennial theme was changed to "Hawaiian Holidays," while the '70s saw a "Good Old Days" nostalgia theme.

Today an agricultural theme is featured each year, and has included "Everything's Coming Up Rosy," a salute to pigs; "Don't Miss the Egg-citement," a salute to the poultry and egg industries; and "Meet Our Main Squeeze," a nod to California's citrus industry.

The modern fair's theme usually coincides with a publicity stunt. In 1991, for instance, a man covered himself with 200,000 honeybees daily during the fair's 12-day salute to bees and honey.

This year's theme was "We're Putting a Bug in Your Ear" and the fair's organizers offered free samples of cooked mealworms, crickets, beetles and other delectable insects for your dining pleasure from Ron Taylor, the "Bug Chef."

Live music has always been a major draw at the fair, and has included everyone from Roy Orbison and Rick Nelson to the Rembrandts and Crystal Gayle. The concerts are free with paid admission.

And of course, there are always the usual rides, food, games and special exhibits to keep any family occupied for an entire day or more. That's why every July Orange Countians leave their video games, TVs and VCRs for a while to enjoy a good old-fashioned day at the fair.

Established in 1892, the Orange County Fair today attracts more than 700,000 people.

THE GREAT ORANGE COUNTY OIL BOOM OF THE 1920S

Like the great plains of Texas and Oklahoma, Orange County was once the site of oil strikes that created instant fortunes and rugged boomtowns.

The first county oil strike was in 1882 in the Brea Canyon area, and led to successful drilling in nearby Fullerton and La Habra. The oil reservoirs in Brea had been expected, though. The crude was seeping from the ground.

But it was the surprise gusher of 1920 in Huntington Beach that literally knocked everyone off their feet.

There were early signs that Huntington Beach had a vast reservoir of oil beneath its surface, but few recognized what those signs meant. In the 1910s, for instance, real estate developers were frustrated in their probes for fresh water in the area. A mixture of water and gas would bubble up instead.

To a geologist, the gaseous water would have been a sign of what lay underneath. To the developers, it was a roadblock to building in the seaside farming community.

In 1918, Standard Oil Company hired a young engineer to study areas of Southern California for oil. Through his studies, he concluded that a mesa near Garfield Avenue and Golden West Street in Huntington Beach was a petroleum-bearing site.

The young man asked his superiors at Standard Oil to drill a well. But the company didn't believe him. Up to this time, oil had been discovered by "wildcatting" — drilling a hole wherever an oilman's intuition was strongest.

But the engineer was persistent, and finally one official relented to drilling a well, if only to prove the novice wrong.

Using a newly developed rotary drill bit that could reach half a mile into the earth, the Standard Oil engineer went to work searching for oil under a field of barley.

On Aug. 3, 1920 people for miles around heard a huge roar. Oil company workers fell to the ground as the gusher spewed oil 200 feet into the air.

The oilmen were unprepared for the find. They funneled the oil over a cliff into some corn fields below. More than 2,000 barrels a day created huge pools of oil over acres of land. Five hundred men with mules and shovels worked feverishly to build a dike to contain the crude.

People travelled from far and wide to see the strike. Because of the noise from the gusher, local schools were closed and students made their way down to the site.

"When the gusher came in, it was like a carnival came to town, or a big fire," said one resident from the time. "Everyone came to watch."

After a week, workers were able to cap the gusher and set up the first oil well in the coastal region of Southern California. The well was called Huntington A-1 and the mesa where it stood became known as Reservoir Hill.

Almost overnight, roughnecks from oilfields around the country descended on the small city. Within a month after the strike, the population jumped from 1,500 to 5,000 residents.

Six months later there were more than 800 producing wells and local farmers were becoming millionaires. Where once they worked the clay ground to grow what they could, many were now leasing the land and moving into mansions.

Each well needed a crew of 30 men who all needed places to eat and sleep. Hotels and restaurants couldn't be built fast enough. In that first year, total income in the city rose from $4,000 to $250,000. By the middle of the decade, the petroleum industry was responsible for the largest payroll in the county.

In 1922, Midway City was built to provide homes for the Huntington Beach oil field employees, midway between the established cities of Santa Ana and Long Beach.

Prior to the oil strike, Huntington Beach had touted itself as a resort town where "there are no saloons or drinking and morality is of the highest order."

That soon changed with the influx of young men from oil states, who brought with them a flood of unsavory characters. Bootleggers sold whiskey, while downtown hotels became brothels and gambling halls.

Con artists also entered the picture after the oil strike. Many would entice investors from Long Beach and Los Angeles by bussing them in for lunch at an oil-drilling site. Little did the investors know the site was usually dry, the oil derrick just a prop. Locals called the endless procession of investors "sucker buses."

The life of the roughneck was a dangerous one. Fires and blowouts were common. If a well caught fire, a roughneck would climb the burning rig while flames were kept away with a high-powered hose.

The worker would attach a line so firemen could pull down the rig in a safe direction. It was a tricky situation. If a rig fell into another, it could set off a domino effect of falling, burning oil derricks.

Blowouts were sometimes worse for people living in close proximity to an oil field. One blowout covered a house with mud, oil and rocks, wrecked the family automobile and covered the lawn with a thick layer of oil. The family sued the oil company.

In 1926 oil company officials decided that a good reserve was located near the ocean, south of 23rd Street. There was an election and Huntington Beach residents voted to open the area to drilling, hoping that the economic good times would continue. By the end of the 20s, only eight blocks of downtown Huntington Beach were legally off-limits to drilling.

By the 30s, "whipstock" or slant drilling was introduced to tap oil resources beneath farms and homes and out into the ocean. Slant-drilling continues to this day, with many derricks camouflaged near residential tracts. Off-shore rigs replaced most of the on-shore oil derricks.

Huntington Beach continues to be one of the top oil-producing cities in California. In fact, half the oil removed from Orange County land has come from the seaside city.

Oil derricks surround the Huntington Beach Grammar School, circa 1925.

How McFadden's Wharf Created Newport Beach

Looking at the city's beautiful waterfront homes and magnificent yachts, it's easy to think Newport Beach has been the crown jewel of Orange County forever.

Actually, some one hundred years ago, the harbor was nothing but a sandbar-filled estuary with not a boat in sight. The natural land-locked harbor was so treacherous, no boat of any size had ever managed to navigate it.

Ships sailed up and down the coast between San Francisco and San Diego, stopping at minor ports along the way to deliver and pick up cargo. Orange County farmers hauled their produce and goods by wagon to Anaheim Landing, or what is today Seal Beach, or to San Pedro, a difficult journey at best.

But in 1870, a hardy, sea-faring man named Capt. S.S. Dunnells successfully steered his flat-bottomed sternwheeler, the Vaquero, into the Bolsa de San Joaquin, as the harbor was called at the time.

Dunnells reported proudly back to San Diego that he had found a "new port," and so Newport Bay was named. Dunnells and a partner, W.H. Abbott, decided to build a wharf at the back of the bay where the Newport Nautical Museum is today.

Farmers and ranchers began bringing their crops and cowhides to the wharf where flat-bottomed scows ferried loads to deep-water ships anchored off-shore.

In 1873 local farmer James McFadden ordered a shipload of Northern California redwood to the wharf so he could fence off his 5,000 acres in Delhi, a town just south of Santa Ana. It seems wild horses were running over everyone's crops, and local farmers purchased every stick of wood McFadden had to spare.

Because of the demand, McFadden sent for a second shipment. When a third load sold before it reached Dunnells' wharf, McFadden decided it was time to go into the lumber business.

On April 19, 1875 he purchased the wharf from Dunnells and renamed it McFadden's Landing. To ensure ships would continue to dock nearby, he enlisted the help of local farmers who drove 25 teams of horses and mules and dredged the harbor at low tide.

Two vessels, the Vaquero and the Twin Sisters, were regular visitors. In 1876 McFadden and his brother Robert had a shallow-draft steamer, the Newport, built for them in San Francisco.

By 1879 large steamers were stopping at the port, dispatching small boats called "lighters" into Newport Bay to pick up cargo at McFadden's Landing. During that year, more than five-million pounds of corn alone left the wharf. Other shipments included barley, wool, dried fruit, honey and beans.

To speed up their operation, the brothers leased an acre of high land from James Irvine behind the wharf. They built a warehouse with a chute so goods could be sent down the 80-foot cliff to the boats below. With this addition, steamships bearing 50-ton cargoes were leaving the bay three times a week.

The bay was still a dangerous place. In 1885 two skiffs were overturned and five men drowned beneath the falling cargo. In 1887 the McFaddens' close friend and harbor pilot Tom Rule drowned while marking the channel for the brothers. That was the last straw.

They applied for federal money to improve the bay, but failed. Government engineers suggested the brothers build a commercial pier on the ocean side of the harbor's long and narrow sandspit.

In August 1888 a wooden wagon bridge was completed that crossed the west end of the bay. For the first time, horse-drawn vehicles and pedestrians could cross from the mainland to the once isolated sandspit. This convinced the McFaddens to organize the Newport Wharf and Lumber Co., and on December 1, 1888 a pier extending 1,300 feet over the ocean was completed.

A barge loaded with the McFaddens' office maneuvered through the bay and the office was installed on the pier. By the end of its first year, 72 vessels had taken cargo, making it one of the busiest wharves in Southern California.

Their wharf was such a success the McFadden brothers purchased 1,000 acres of Newport Beach from the state at a modest $1 an acre. Today the land would stretch from 9th Street to 40th, plus Lido and Balboa islands.

Wishing to modernize the transportation of goods to the pier, the McFaddens started the Santa Ana & Newport Railroad Co.

By January 12, 1889, an 11-mile road bed had been graded to Santa Ana and the track laying began at both ends. Ties, rails, and four flat cars were shipped to the pier. By 1891 the first passengers and cargo took the 40-minute trip on tracks that started in Santa Ana and ended on the pier itself.

In two years, the McFaddens' railroad company was doing a half-million dollar freight business. Their passenger side of the business was doing well, also, as they sold 50-cent tickets to beachgoers and those taking boats to Catalina Island.

The McFaddens began selling cottages to summer vacationers as well as camping sites for $8 a month to accommodate these early sun-worshipers. By 1896 there were a hundred homes and other city landmarks, including a post office, the Newport and Sharp's hotels, a school and a pavilion.

Devout Scotch Presbyterians, the McFaddens refused to run the railroad on Sunday, which allowed local residents a chance to enjoy a walk on the pier. There was no railing, so fishermen were on their own when reeling in their catches.

Several times the Southern Pacific Railroad attempted to purchase the Santa Ana-Newport line, but the McFaddens emphatically refused the offers. In 1899, the brothers decided to sell the concern to sugar farmer J. Ross Clark of Los Alamitos. But Clark was just a front man for the Southern Pacific, and the McFaddens sold the rest of their beach property in disgust.

An era ended in 1907 when the last steamer sailed from the pier loaded with goods. But the McFaddens, and the pier they built, had introduced Newport Beach to the world.

The McFadden Pier at Newport Beach, terminus of the Pacific Red Cars

ORANGE COUNTY - OSTRICH CAPITAL OF THE NATION

When people think of Orange County, the phrase "ostrich capital of the nation" doesn't generally come to mind. But at one time in the not-so-distant past, we were just that.

Shortly before the turn-of-the-century, the nation's women had decided it was the height of fashion to adorn their hats with ostrich plumes. They also used the plumes for collars, muffs and for cooling themselves with ostrich feather fans.

A single plume could fetch up to $15 from a high-society lady in London, New York or Chicago. In 1882 Billie Frantz, a successful chicken farmer in Anaheim, saw an opportunity.

Frantz journeyed to San Francisco where he was introduced to a small flock of ostriches, smuggled out of South Africa the year before. South Africa was the only place in the world raising ostriches for their plumes and charged a hefty export duty.

Frantz learned the birds had modest needs, living on a diet of grass, grain, weeds and gravel (that's right, gravel). A full-grown bird yielded four hundred feathers, weighing a total of one and half pounds.

After some quick arithmetic, Frantz was sold on starting "the craziest chicken ranch in California." He raised $30,000 from investors, founded the California Ostrich Company, and remodeled his farm to accommodate poultry weighing 300 pounds apiece.

Naturalist Dr. C.J. Sketchley was hired to supervise the birds' transportation and care and feeding at their new home. On March 22, 1883, the unlikely band of immigrants arrived in Anaheim on the noon train.

Visitors came by the hundreds to see Frantz' new tenants, and the farmer learned the birds' tastes were more extravagant than claimed. During the first week, they snatched and swallowed six earrings, a dozen brooches and several hatpins (sometimes with the hats attached) from terrified on-lookers.

Dr. Sketchly explained to Frantz that ostriches eat jewelry, bones and gravel to grind up food. Future visitors were warned of the birds' appetites and were charged 50 cents for a peek through a high fence.

The novelty eventually wore off and the farm settled down to the business of breeding. When the first eggs were laid, Frantz invited 10 of his investors to lunch. One egg, boiled for an hour and a half, fed the entire bunch.

Frantz and his co-patriots found plucking the big birds could be a hazardous endeavor. They discovered the ostrich had a kick as strong as a mule's, and could easily injure them. To keep the birds calm, a canvas bag was tied over their heads while one man held the bird and another plucked.

The dozen hens in the original group did not breed as fast as Frantz had hoped, and the birds would occasionally peck each other to death. To increase his profits, he began selling hatchlings at $450 apiece and the ostrich industry spread throughout California, Arizona and Nevada.

Four farms opened in the county, including a successful operation run by Edward Atherton in Fullerton. He also had problems with tourists, though. One day a visitor's dog began chasing the birds and one jumped a four-foot fence and didn't stop running for 15 miles.

One wild moment in the county's ostrich history occurred when a wagonload of the birds from Edwin Cawston's La Habra farm tipped over, setting a dozen ostriches loose in the community. For days, residents were amused at the site of ranch hands chasing the freed birds around town.

In 1896, Frantz considered the potential of the ostrich as a racing animal. He started training two of the tamer birds, Napoleon and Bonaparte, to pull a small cart. It wasn't easy since the pair would often stop and sit down in the road for no particular reason.

Frantz raced the birds at the Santa Ana Race Track and beat horses and bicyclists. He soon took the show on the road, doing exhibition races at fairs, carnivals and circuses throughout the Southwest.

But one day while feeding the birds Napoleon gave Frantz a vicious kick that nearly killed him. He retired his riding crop and sold his entire flock of birds except for two. He started growing oranges on his farm, and later found his last two birds dead from choking on too many oranges.

With the arrival of the automobile, other ostrich farmers were faring no better. Seems that windy auto travel and ostrich feather hats were not a good match. By 1922, the last ostrich farm in Orange County closed its gates.

So ended one of the fowlest chapters in Orange County history.

Billie Frantz with Napoleon, 'the first racing ostrich in the U.S.'

ORANGE PLAZA RETAINS TURN-OF-CENTURY LOOK

Take a walk through the Orange Plaza and you feel that you're walking back in time.

With brick-and-mortar buildings lining the streets and a small park with a fountain in the center of the intersection, the downtown area has the appearance of 1895 rather than 1995. You can easily imagine a simpler time when the plaza was filled with townsfolk taking casual strolls on warm summer evenings.

"Orange has the county's only old downtown center still intact," said local historian Phil Brigandi. "Everything you see is the way it would have looked in 1915 or 1920."

"Other cities may have old buildings, but they can never have the impact of a whole row that you find at the Plaza," Brigandi said. "There's a real ambiance there that grows on you."

Although common in towns of the East and Midwest, the circular park in the center of the city's downtown intersection is unique in the county, with an interesting tale behind it.

The park and fountain came about more than 100 years ago when a group of residents decided to literally clean-up the town.

During the 1870s, it seems the intersection of Chapman Avenue and Glassell Street had become an eyesore, with livestock herded through it by local ranchers. It didn't help matters when merchants set water troughs around so farmers would leave their livestock and purchase their wares. The ranchers would often dump their trash during their stay as well.

In the city's original plans, the founding fathers had donated the intersection to the public. In 1883 residents reclaimed the area, placing a barbed-wire fence around the intersection to keep out sheep and cattle. They began to raise funds for a park through the sale of baked goods and fruits.

Their dream was to place a fountain in the center of the park, but they were short of the fountain's $585 price tag. The residents came up with an unusual solution — they produced a five-act play called "The Plaza," a comedy that satirized the city and its citizens, and especially the real estate buying frenzy that was hitting the area. Despite poking fun at local residents, the play was a success and the fountain money was raised.

In 1887 the renovation of the Plaza finally began. Many townspeople donated trees and seeds and lots of time and labor. Later that year a beautiful three-tiered fountain topped by a bird which spouted water from its bill was installed.

In the 1930s the fountain was moved next to a public swimming pool in Hart Park during a WPA project. Many locals remember wading in the fountain as toddlers.

The fountain was restored and moved in 1981 in front of the Orange Civic Center, a few hundred feet away from its old home in the Plaza park. A WPA-built fountain stands in the park today.

The area surrounding the Plaza park features one of the largest concentrations of historical structures in Southern California. Many of the buildings were built from the 1880s to the 1930s and feature rarely seen columns, elaborate cornices, scrolls and fancy brickwork.

In 1982 the area was officially listed as a historic district by the National Register of Historic Places, the country's highest level of historic designation.

Among those historic places is Watson's Drugs and Soda Fountain, the oldest drugstore in the county and the oldest ongoing business in Orange. First established in 1899, it is still a favorite gathering place of local residents.

Outside the original Orange Daily News building is a plaque commemorating the site of the city's first orange trees planted in the 1890s. The city would later be covered with orange groves.

Then there's the Masonic Lodge, originally the site of Campbell's Opera House where only plays and speeches were held, not operas. The Masons have been tenants there since 1923.

Other notable sites include the First National Bank building, the first bank in the city, with its high Corinthian columns; the Mediterranean-style Orange Building and Loan Association building, constructed in the mid-20s and the site of USO shows during World War II; and the original Orange Theater building, opened in 1929, where local residents first saw the "talkies" in the extravagantly decorated interior.

Today the Plaza attracts people from all over Southern California for its many antique shops, which fit in perfectly with the turn-of-the-century atmosphere.

Those who live in and around the area are passionate about keeping the historic buildings, like 31-year resident Ann Milowicki. She chose to live in the city because of the downtown area.

"It reminded me of my hometown back East," Milowicki said. "When I saw the Plaza, I knew Orange would be a good place to live."

The Orange Plaza in the 1920s

SHAKE SHACK ON PCH - A COUNTY ROADSIDE INSTITUTION

If you've ever driven Pacific Coast Highway near Corona del Mar, you must have seen it. Maybe you've even stopped by.

It's a bright yellow roadside stand overlooking the ocean that has served locals and tourists delicious date shakes and magnificent views for decades.

Known today as the Crystal Cove Shake Shack, it's also been called the Date Shack and Sunshine Cove. Until recently, when developers began grading for homes across the highway, it was surrounded by undeveloped property.

Everytime I've passed by, it has always seemed a miracle to me the stand had survived. So one recent afternoon I stopped by to uncover the story behind the shack.

Pulling off PCH, I first noticed that a paved parking lot had replaced the dirt, dust and mud patrons once encountered. And the shack itself had been remodeled to look brand new.

I remembered the stand mostly as a funky, hippie establishment by the sea with strange health foods like tofu and alfalfa sprouts on the menu.

Today it serves hearty sandwiches and shakes, with a diverse clientele eating outside and enjoying the view, including surfers with their hair still wet from cutting up the waves, businessmen on lunch break, families from Iowa, couples on Harleys and bicycle warriors pedaling up the coast.

I introduced myself to Mike Flamson, the Shake Shack's current manager. The busy lunch hour was just ending, but Mike seemed more serene than Buddha. Who wouldn't be relaxed, I guess, working next to the sparkling Pacific all day?

For the past five years, the Flamson family of Corona del Mar has leased the lot from the State of California. The state purchased the bluff and all the property below from the Irvine Company in the late 70s and made it part of the Crystal Cove State Park.

"They were going to close this place down a few years ago when they widened PCH," Flamson said. "But they got so much flak from the community, they re-aligned the highway to avoid the shack."

The state put some conditions on anyone who wanted to operate the stand, though. It had to be refurbished, remain painted yellow and continue to serve date shakes.

As far as anyone can tell, the shack was built in 1944. It was made entirely of corrugated steel over a post frame.

Not much is known about the early years of the shack's operation. No one even knows the name of the builder. However, it can be identified in aerial photographs taken in the 1950s.

In the 60s and early 70s, it was called the Date Shack and sold fresh fruit and juices. The operator at the time sub-leased it from an elderly man, who may have been the shack's builder.

In 1974, Virginia McKinney began renting the Date Shack from the Irvine Company. She changed the name to the Sunshine Cove and put up the once familiar signs with orange and yellow suns at either end of the parking lot.

Known as Mrs. Sunshine, McKinney added many of the natural health foods she served in her Laguna Beach restaurant. And in addition to the date shakes, she introduced exotic shakes that featured almonds, peanut butter, mangos, papaya and bananas.

In 1989, McKinney's lease with the state expired. According to state law, any new lease had to be opened to the public, and McKinney's bid was too low. Rumors circulated that the lease had been granted to a fast-food chain that would bulldoze the shack. Local residents pleaded with public officials to keep the building intact.

The lease had been awarded to the Flamsons, and rumors about the fast-food chain being built were unfounded. Today, the shack is busier and more prosperous than ever. It also stays open during weekdays in the winter, which it never had before.

Once Mike Flamson had filled me in on its history, I had to ask one question — what's in those famous date shakes?

All he would tell me is that his wife played with the original mixture of dates and vanilla ice cream sprinkled with nutmeg until customers gave it their vote of approval.

"We get customers who have come here for years for nothing but the date shakes," Flamson said. "We've tried not to mess with success."

I spoke with some of the shack's patrons, including Tim Hodges of Newport Beach, who had stopped by with his wife and daughter for a date shake on their way to San Diego.

"To tell you the truth, this is the first time I've been here in 25 years," Hodges said. "I used to come here after surfing with my friends. A lot of them used to work here, too."

Even though Hodges hasn't been by the shack in awhile, he hopes the landmark stays around forever.

"It's a throwback to the old Newport Coast, which is disappearing pretty fast," he said. "I'd miss it if it wasn't here."

The Shake Shack has been a favorite stop along PCH for more than 50 years.

The Great County Silver Rush of the 1870s

Nearly 30 years after the Gold Rush of 1849, Orange County experienced its own "Silver Rush," complete with swarms of prospectors and a miners' boomtown.

In October 1877 local businessmen Hank Smith and Bill Curry were deer-hunting in the Santa Ana Mountains when they came upon blue and white quartz rocks scattered on a canyon floor.

The two men believed the blue and white streaks were silver deposits. Gathering a few of the rocks, the men took the ore to an assay office in Los Angeles. Their hunches were confirmed. It was silver, second only to gold in its value as a precious metal.

Spurred by visions of discovering a vein like Nevada's great Comstock Lode, the two men went back and prospected the entire upper end of the canyon, eventually staking a claim and building a tunnel 50-feet into the canyon's walls. They named the mine the Southern Belle.

Not surprisingly, their secret didn't last long. The story broke in a big way just a few weeks later in the Los Angeles Evening News.

"The silver is there in immense quantities," the Evening News wrote. "Old miners from the silver mines of Nevada pronounce them as rich as those of any state, excepting none."

Within days of the article more than 300 prospectors swarmed into the Santa Ana Mountains from all over the state.

The prospectors rented horses and wagons from stables in Santa Ana and Anaheim and raced over make-shift dirt roads into the hills, staking claims along Santiago Creek and in the canyon walls. Wherever you looked, there were men swinging pick-axes in a frantic search for a silver vein beneath the ground.

Before the silver discovery, the area had been known as Canada de la Madera — Canyon of the Timber, named by the Spanish for its dense woods. During the years following California's statehood in 1850, the canyon was home to only a handful of shacks where residents kept bees and raised goats.

But the silver changed all that. By the summer of 1878, a mining village had sprung up at the lower end of the canyon. P.A. Clark, a real estate man from Anaheim, laid out the townsite and named it Silverado. Canada de la Madera quickly became known as Silverado Canyon.

Population in Silverado rose to 1,500 residents in its first few months of existence. Lots were sold at fantastic prices. Soon there were three hotels, three stores, two blacksmiths shops and a school. There were also seven saloons and at least as many preachers.

Three stages ran daily from Santa Ana to the remote town, and two from Los Angeles. Seats were at a premium. Another five or six large wagons filled with ore rumbled out of the mountains daily.

Despite the construction, most miners preferred to "tent out" near their mines with names such as the Old Gray Back Lode, the Alpha, and the Montezuma. The most famous of the mines was the Blue Light.

In 1880 a deputy U.S. marshal named J.D. Dunlap was sent to arrest a Mexican outlaw hiding in the mountains. Dunlap never succeeded in apprehending the fugitive, but did catch mining fever.

He put a crew to work and found some silver-rich ore that helped spread the news of the county's silver discovery. Dunlap succeeded in shipping smelter to San Francisco at a net profit of $140 per ton, or $28,000.

Hearing of the find, a group of eastern financiers formed the New York Mining Company and purchased all the property not already staked out by prospectors. They spent a sizable fortune on their development, but only mined a few hundred dollars worth of ore.

The Blue Light Mine still held the greatest promise for a big pay-off. Once Dunlap thought he had struck the Mother Lode, he pierced the whole side of the canyon with tunnels.

But what appeared to be rich veins disappeared after just a few feet and couldn't be traced any further. Time and again Dunlap and his crew would strike a sparkling white vein, congratulate themselves on their new-found riches, only to start searching for another.

Other miners found the same luck. They couldn't have known that they were digging in earthquake country where the bedrock had been broken-up by countless quakes over the centuries, leaving the silver vein virtually untraceable.

Soon the wagons filled with ore were leaving the canyon three times a week instead of the daily runs. Then there were only two runs a week, then one. The hotel, stores and saloon began boarding up.

By 1883, the boomtown of Silverado went bust, becoming a ghost town like so many other mining towns from the Old West. Remnants of the town and the mines can still be found in the Santa Ana Mountains.

The one lasting legacy of the great Orange County silver rush?

The area will be forever known as Silverado Canyon.

The Blue Light Mine held the most promise to miners searching for silver ore.

IT'S A 'SOLDIER'S LIFE' AT ANAHEIM MILITARY SCHOOL

There are a lot of elementary schools in Orange County, but my guess is there's only one with a 12-year-old brigade commander.

That would be St. Catherine's Military School in Anaheim. Founded in 1889, the all-boys academy is the oldest continuously operating school in Orange County and the last military school in Southern California.

To most people, myself included, the term "military school" conjures up images of incorrigible youngsters living under harsh discipline. To hear the real story, I recently visited the school and talked with spokesperson Ms. Chris Ragon.

"It's true that a military school is not your run-of-the-mill elementary," Ragon said. "Our school combines the traditions of the military with learning."

"This means we have uniforms, merit programs, marching and drills, ranking among students, and inspection of clothes and dorms."

The classes are taught by nuns who live on campus. However, the school is not a replica of Boys Town, she said.

"We don't accept kids who are too wild," Ragon said. "We're not the last step before Juvenile Hall."

Parents enroll their sons for a variety of reasons, she said. Some like the school's academic reputation, while others want the structured environment for their sons with attention-deficit disorders.

Families from Mexico, Thailand, France and other countries send their sons to study English at the school. Since the academy has dorms, the youngsters can be housed on-campus throughout the school year.

"A few students are here because they have an interest in a military career," Ragon said. "Many of St. Catherine's graduates have gone on to West Point and other military universities."

St. Catherine's began as an all-girls school by the Dominican Sisters of Mission San Jose. But there just weren't enough students in the area to fill its classrooms. So two years after it opened, the school became an orphanage.

By the early 1900s, the orphanage was housing only boys. The facility was crowded, says Ragon, because at the time children were often taken away from single parents until they re-married or found gainful employment.

While the ranks of the orphaned boys grew, the sisters began looking around for a way to provide a male influence at the institution. In 1923 they asked the Boy Scouts for assistance, but they declined, not wanting to be affiliated with a specific religion.

The determined sisters then asked retired military men living nearby for help. A few agreed to set up and oversee a program for the boys based on military traditions. In 1925, the St. Catherine's Military Academy was officially opened.

Today there are 180 students from kindergarten to eighth grade. Most of the students return to their families in the evening, but about 45 students spend the week on campus and return home on the weekends. Another 20 are "seven-day" cadets who spend the entire school year on campus, only returning to their homes on Christmas, Easter and summer vacation.

Surprisingly, only half the students are Catholic. The other students come from many religious backgrounds, including Buddhist, Jehovah Witness, Mormon, Judaism and Muslim.

Students are taught about all the world's religions, though they are required to attend a Catholic Mass each week in the school's chapel. The non-Catholics are encouraged to pray privately during the service.

"The sisters are not here to convert students to Catholicism," Ragon said. "All religions share common goals for humanity and that's what we stress."

The on-site chapel is a story unto itself. Inside are three beautiful works of art by John DeRosen. On one wall is a 90-foot mural titled "The Descent of Truth." It depicts 24 Catholic saints, from Joan of Arc and Thomas Aquinas to the school's namesake, St. Catherine of Siena.

On the other side of the chapel are stained-glass windows showing the miracles of Christ, while behind the altar is another mural depicting the Crucifixion.

Inside the school's cafeteria are photos from 1955 when Charlton Heston was on campus filming "The Private Life of Major Benson." The movie company used the school's cadets in the film and compensated the school by building a new athletic field.

Other on-site facilities include an indoor pool and gymnasium, barber shop and music room where piano is taught to all age groups.

Alumni often send their own sons to the school, Ragon said. For instance, the current brigade commander, the top rank among cadets, is the fourth generation in his family to attend St. Catherine's. His great-grandfather was a cadet in the 1920s.

Other alumni visit and give talks to the cadets about how the school helped them in their lives.

The school's enrollment peaked during the 1960s, and the student numbers have been hurt by economic conditions, Ragon said.

But with today's parents looking for ways to improve learning and discipline, Ragon believes St. Catherine's will continue to serve as an educational alternative for many years to come.

St. Catherine's Military Academy in Anaheim, circa 1927

THE BALBOA BAY CLUB - THE HOST OF THE COAST

Let me admit it right from the start — I have always wanted to be a member of the exclusive Balboa Bay Club.

Through the years it would've been great to share a joke with comic Joey Bishop, drink a beer with Irish actor Victor McLaglin, chat with visiting sports legends, or swap fishing stories with John Wayne.

The Balboa Bay Club, or "the BBC" to members, got its start when the bay wasn't much more than a few docks, some abandoned Navy schooners and lots of sand bars.

It was 1946 when Manhattan real estate mogul Ken Kendall purchased a home on the bay. Kendall owned a cruiser, the Verona II, and would frequently moor it near his Lido Isle lot and hold parties on the stern in summer. One evening, Kendall kept staring at an empty beach across the bay.

"You know, there's really nothing for people to do down here, especially in the evening," Kendall said to a friend. "Just think what you could do with that piece of property over there."

Kendall had established a yacht club in Long Island years before and had set his mind to bringing East Coast style to Newport Beach. He invited two local developers, Hadd Ring and Thomas Henderson, to take a walk on the property. The three men sat on a log and discussed the kind of club they would develop.

"We wanted to build a family-oriented club that reflected the elite lifestyle we believed would someday come to this area," Ring later recalled. "The club would provide the very finest in hospitality, dining, entertainment and sports."

Kendall and his partners leased the land from the city and began selling memberships from a hamburger stand on Pacific Coast Highway — a humble start if ever there was one. All they had to offer were sketches of what was planned for the site showing a swimming pool, bar, tennis courts and piers.

Somehow Kendall found 100 associates, neighbors and passers-by to purchase memberships at $100 apiece. This became his start-up capital for the BBC.

Opened in 1948, the Balboa Bay Club immediately became the center of good times for Orange County's rich and famous.

"There was a party everywhere," recalled one early member. "I lived in 'Alimony Row' — they were beach cottages where members stayed whenever they quarreled with their wives."

Another member recalled hosting a party the night before he left for Tokyo on a business trip. The revelry continued through the morning and into the next evening. The club member took his plane flight and, upon his return two weeks later, discovered the party was still going strong without him.

The BBC also became a favorite fun zone for Hollywood celebrities, including Humphrey Bogart and Loren Bacall, Lana Turner, William Holden, Dorothy Lamour, David Niven, Bing Crosby and Sonjie Heinie. It was a place to unwind without fear of meeting overzealous fans or a critical press.

There was a serious side to many of the BBC's social functions. The club's members began the first fund-raising events for what would eventually become Hoag Hospital. The right wing of the hospital was referred to as the Bay Club Annex for years after it was built.

Many county charities got their start at the BBC, including the Assistance League, the Children's Home Society, the League for Crippled Children and the Orange County Philharmonic Society.

Politicians were always regular visitors to the club, especially Republican stalwarts Barry Goldwater and Ronald Reagan. But both sides of the political coin have been represented in the past. In 1960, for example, there were two major political fund-raisers at the club — one for Richard Nixon, the other for John F. Kennedy.

During the 1960s one celebrity who began attending BBC events became associated with the club more than any other — John Wayne. He is remembered by many club members as having a heart as big as the outdoors. Wayne never missed a Christmas party where club members served dinner to the BBC's employees, and he would always stop and sign autographs.

The club also became a favorite spot for big names in amateur and professional sports, and before long championship tennis tournaments were being held at the BBC.

As one member put it, "During its history, the Balboa Bay Club has been the Southern California headquarters for nearly every sport except polo. We'll have that, too, when they teach horses to swim."

The BBC's annual "Sportsman of the Year" banquet has honored the top names in sport for decades, including John Wooden, Don Drysdale, Dan Gurney and Bill Shoemaker.

You name it, the Balboa Bay Club has made a party out of it. Maybe that's why it's known by the rich and famous throughout the country as the "Host of the Coast."

The Duke holds court at a Balboa Bay Club function.

SURF'S UP AT HB SURF MUSEUM

There aren't many museums in the world where visitors dressed in surf trunks and flip-flops can be overheard muttering things like "Stoking!" and "Radical!"

But this is no ordinary museum. It's the Huntington Beach International Surfing Museum. Resembling a surfer's dream attic, the museum is a suitably laid-back tribute to the sport's pioneers and to the California beach culture that has been exported to the four corners of the globe.

The tiny 2,000-square-foot museum is the only one in the world officially accredited by the International Surfing Association. Hawaii may have bigger waves and its native Polynesians may have invented the sport, but the state doesn't have a museum dedicated to surfing.

How Huntington Beach grabbed the initiative is credited to Natalie Kotsch, a local real estate agent who never surfed a wave in her life.

Kotsch's Pier Realty was located on Main Street in downtown Huntington Beach. During the mid-1980s she became friends with some of the city's surfing legends who would pass by on their way to the beach.

One of those legends was George Farquhar. After his death at age 71, Kotsch learned that his trophies, photos, books and other surfing memorabilia were being dispersed among family members around the country.

"Panic set in when I heard about his mementos leaving the area," Kotsch said. "I knew those treasures would probably just sit in someone's garage and deteriorate. That was our city's history."

A solution came to her while on a car trip to Sacramento. Looking through a AAA tourbook, she discovered there was no mention of her hometown.

"I felt we had to have at least one significant thing we could say was in Huntington Beach," she said. "It occurred to me there should be a surfing museum."

With its eight miles of beaches and several major surfing competitions, including the OP Surf Tournament every August, Kotsch believed the city was a natural for a museum dedicated to surfing. And where else was surfing a varsity sport at the local high school?

Kotsch formed a museum board and its members held their first meeting in 1987. A year and a half later, a small temporary exhibit opened on Walnut Street. When downtown redevelopment brought the wrecking ball down on the building six months later, the board searched for a new museum site.

The real estate agent went to the city council and got a grant from the redevelopment agency and the free use of an abandoned downtown building. Aided by additional private contributions, the non-profit, volunteer-run museum opened its doors at 411 Olive St. on June 16, 1990.

Today the museum draws thousands of visitors every year from all over the world and from every state in the union.

A bust of Duke Kahanamoku, "the father of surfing," greets visitors at the entrance. The Duke was an Olympic swimmer from Waikiki who is credited with popularizing surfing. On an exhibition tour in 1916, he introduced the sport to the San Diego area and returned in the early 1920s to surf beneath the Huntington Beach Pier.

If you're lucky, museum curator Ann Beasley (she likes to be called a 'dudette') will be there to show you a rare artifact — the original hood ornament from the Duke's car depicting a surfer riding a wave.

Next is a display of those who have been inducted into the Surfers Walk of Fame. This is a new wrinkle the museum began two years ago that gives surfing legends a nameplate in the sidewalk at the corner of Pacific Coast Highway and Main Street.

The museum's first inductees include "Endless Summer" filmmaker Bruce Brown, surfboard-maker Robert August (also featured in "Endless Summer"), '70s surf great Mark Richards and Joyce Hoffman, a trail-blazing woman surfer.

An entire wall is dedicated to surf music and includes Dick Dale's first electric guitar, original concert posters and album covers from the Beach Boys, the Surfaris, the Fantastic Baggys and dozens of other bands.

Nearby there's poster art and videotapes from a number of surf movies where visitors can view portions of movies like "Beach Blanket Bingo" or "Ride the Wild Surf."

Another exhibit shows the early days of surfing in Hawaii. Illustrations from the 1700s show the native Polynesians surfing "au naturel" in the waves. According to the display, the Polynesians used surfing as a place to meet and court. Even the marriage ceremony took place while surfing.

One wall is dedicated to a few Huntington Beach surfers known as the "Hole in the Wall Gang." During the late '70s, this motley band of older surfers dominated the sport, eventually winning the World Team Championship in 1977.

Considering it operates with no grants or paid staff, the Huntington Beach International Surfing Museum is a treat for anyone who grew up in Southern California. With just a $2 donation, you really can't go wrong.

Curator Ann Beasley with a vintage longboard

How Orange County Cities Got Their Names

In a way, cities are like people. They are given names when they are born that forever identify them. And there's usually a good story on how the name was chosen.

In Orange County, cities have got their names through poker games, from railroad men and through local legends. Following are some of the more interesting stories behind city names.

Anaheim — When this small German immigrant community began growing grapes in the region, they decided it was time to have a name for their settlement.

At a meeting of the Vineyard Society in 1858 a vote was taken on three of the most popular monikers: Annaheim, Annagau and Weinheim. With no decided majority on the first vote, a second ballot was taken.

Annaheim won with 20 votes, with Annagau a close second with 18. Annaheim is translated from German to mean "home by the Santa Anna," referring to the Santa Ana River.

A year later, the Vineyard Society dropped the extra 'n' to have the name coincide with the Spanish spelling for Ann.

Brea — In the 1880s people from Pomona and the Santa Ana Valley would come to Canada de la Brea, or Canyon of the Tar, to cut chunks of the oil-soaked earth from canyon walls. They would use the tar for heating their homes and waterproofing their roofs.

In 1891 a Pacific Electric rail line was installed and a small station and town sprang up. The community was named Randolph, after the railroad man who chose the site for the station.

When the city was incorporated in 1911, the railroad man had long since left. The residents renamed the city Brea to recognize the area's origins and publicize its booming oil business.

Buena Park — So many stories have been told how Buena Park was named, it begins to sound like the old "Telephone" game. Tell a story long enough to enough people, and nobody knows the truth in the end.

The most straightforward explanation involves city founder James Whitaker. It's said Whitaker named the city "Boone Park" in 1886 after his hometown in Boone County, Ill. However, early residents asked Whitaker to acknowledge the area's Spanish heritage by renaming it Buena Park. Whitaker complied.

This version is supported by reports of a few old-timers who pronounced the city's name 'Boon-a' Park.

Fountain Valley — For years, the Fountain Valley and Huntington Beach area was known as Gospel Swamp, named for the evangelical preachers who held revival meetings in a marshland that stretched to the ocean.

When the community got its first post office in 1899, residents wanted to call the city Fountain Valley for the many artesian wells dug by farmers. Another California town already claimed that name, so the residents decided on Talbert, after Tom Talbert the Postmaster General.

When the city was incorporated in 1957, residents reinstated the Fountain Valley name when a new search of city names did not turn up a duplicate in the state. Also, the residents wanted the city and the Fountain Valley School District to share the same name.

Fullerton — In the late 1880s the Santa Fe Railroad began choosing townsites around Southern California for stations to support the rail line.

In 1887 Santa Fe's George Fullerton chose the future site of a city in northern Orange County. Real estate developers George Amerige and his brother wanted to name the town after him. But he declined, mostly for reasons of modesty.

Mr. Fullerton left town for a few days. Upon his return, he learned the developers and his railroad co-workers went ahead and named the town after him in his absence.

Lake Forest — This newer Orange County city is one of the few that was named by many of its current residents.

During a vote on incorporation in 1990, voters were asked to choose between three possible new city names — Lake Forest, El Toro and Rancho Canada.

There were some heated battles between residents on this one. Two Lake Forest homeowners' associations preferred their titles, while longtime residents wanted the more traditional El Toro.

According to legend, the name "El Toro" was attributed to a charging bull who turned away from a Spanish missionary standing in its path, praying for divine protection.

The Lake Forest contingent won out by a mere 400 votes. In case you were wondering, there is a man-made lake in the city and a sycamore forest planted by a few of the original settlers.

Orange — In 1875 the founders of Orange were trying to decide on a name for their new city. Albert Chapman wanted "Lemon" and Andrew Glassell favored "Orange," a third gentleman pushed for "Olive," and a fourth liked the sound of "Walnut."

The four men played one poker hand for the privilege of naming the community. Glassell won.

Contrary to popular wisdom, his choice had nothing to do with the groves that would cover the area in future years. The winner's birthplace had been Orange County, Va.

To show there were no hard feelings, the suggested names from the three other players were affixed to streets in the new town of Orange.

El Modena — This unincorporated community near Orange is not named after a city in Mexico as some believe.

The area was actually named by an Italian immigrant in the 1880s for his hometown of Modena, Italy. However, the post office protested that Modena would be confused with two other California cities, Modesto and Madera.

The residents compromised by adding the Spanish prefix 'El.' However, no one realized a mistake — they had used the masculine 'el' with the feminine 'Modena.' The name remained grammatically incorrect.

This city was founded by successful gold miner Columbus Tustin.

DORY FISHERMEN DRAWN TO ROMANCE OF THE SEA

Through the early morning mist in the waters off Newport Beach, a century-old tradition of men returning from the sea is underway.

It's the Dory Fishing Fleet coming ashore near the Newport Pier with another day's catch, as they have been doing since before the pier was even built in the late 1880s.

What drives these men to leave in the night and brave the surf to fish much the way humans have done for thousands of years?

Louis Marberry, who has been working with the dory fishermen for more than 25 years, said it's the romance of the doryman's life and not the money that continues to draw these few hardy souls.

"We've had boats turn over in the water when the ocean gets rough," Marberry said. "This job is definitely not for everyone."

However, the customers at the Dory Village seem to appreciate the dorymen's labors. Harriet Parsons said she drives in with her husband from Anaheim twice a week to purchase fish here.

"I think the dory fishermen are a wonderful institution," Parsons said. "It reminds everyone of what the old days were like. It's also the one place where you know the fish is fresh."

Customers begin gathering at the Dory Village adjacent to the pier when the boats come in at 8 a.m. The catch is small, as has often been the case in recent years, and is made up of mostly mackerel and rock cod.

The "village" is a weather-beaten, beachfront wooden structure made up of a dozen little rooms and replicas of the old wooden rowboats the early dory fishermen used. A wooden sculpture called the Old Doryman stands on top of the structure, watching over the fleet.

While it looks ancient, most of the village was built by the fishermen a few years ago when the pier was remodeled.

The dorymen's story begins in 1888 when James McFadden completed construction of the original pier. At the time there were already dozens of men in V-shaped hull fishing boats called "dories" heading out into the ocean every day and selling their catch along the beach.

To allow the men to continue their livelihood, McFadden sublet the area next to the pier for use by the commercial fishermen.

However, there were certain conditions attached which still apply today. All the fish sold at the dorymen's area must be caught by dory boats going out through the surf and returning through the surf. The fish must also be sold the same day they're caught.

Although McFadden's 100-year lease for the pier wasn't to expire until 1991, the city of Newport Beach designated the Dory Village a historic site in 1969, saving it from potential demolition.

While outboard motors have replaced oars, the fish are caught in the same way they have for years, with long lines of baited hooks and small nets dropped from the boats.

What has changed is how the fish are found. Modern electronics such as deep-reading video sonar and global positioning system (GPS) satellite navigation help the dory crews target schools of fish from Catalina Island to Oceanside.

How does someone become a dory fisherman?

The dory fleet works as a cooperative, and all must abide by the democratically decided rules. When a member leaves, the fishermen vote on accepting the newest member. Each man pays a fee for the use of the village and the area to launch his boat.

Marberry said several of his nephews have been dorymen. It's a hard way to make a living, he said, but it can be done. A few of the obstacles include government quotas on the number of fish they can catch and the declining numbers of fish in local waters.

"Used to be you could drop your line in the water next to the pier and get your 350-pound quota," Marberry said. "Today, if you want to catch fish you have to go a long way — some travel up to 40 miles."

Marberry said most of the catch during the week is sold to local restaurants, while the Dory Village is often jammed with customers on weekends.

"We're really more of a tourist attraction than a fish market these days," Marberry said.

So the next time you're savoring a favorite fish dish, raise your glass and toast the dory fishermen of Newport Beach.

The dory fishermen have been a familiar sight in Newport Beach since the 1800s.

THE RENDEZVOUS BALLROOM - THE PLACE TO BE IN OC

For longtime residents of Orange County, Aug. 7, 1966 will forever be remembered as the day the music died.

For in the early morning hours of that day, the historic Rendezvous Ballroom in Newport Beach burned to the ground. Nothing was left but ashes, scorched brick and some incredible musical memories.

Located on the oceanfront of the Balboa Peninsula, the old building had seen it all — from the Big Band sounds of Glenn Miller, Tommy Dorsey and Benny Goodman, to the innovative music of local jazz great Stan Kenton, to the birth of the surf sound by Dick Dale and the Deltones.

For decades it was simply known as "The Place" by young revelers who would spend their Spring breaks sun-tanning on the beach all day and dancing at the Rendezvous all night.

The legendary Orange County nightspot can trace its beginnings to a tiny dance floor in the back of a popular Balboa eatery called the Green Dragon Cafe. It was there that two of the cafe's regulars, Roy Burlingame and Harry Tudor, dreamed of building a ballroom that would rival the dance hall in the Balboa Pavilion.

Burlingame, president of the Balboa Amusement Co., decided to build the beachfront ballroom in 1928 at a cost of $200,000. Tudor, who became known as "Pop" to young concert-goers, was the facility's first manager.

Designed by architect Milo Berrenson, the Rendezvous covered half a city block between Palm and Washington streets. The two-story hall resembled a huge Hollywood sound stage rather than an ornate ballroom, and featured a mezzanine and balcony.

The 12,000-square-foot dance floor could easily accommodate 1,500 couples. The ballroom also had a 64-foot long soda fountain on the ground floor and a smaller soda fountain upstairs surrounded by 50 sofas.

The Rendezvous made its debut on March 24, 1928 when The Concordias with Carol Lofner conducting played its first number — "Avalon."

But the first incarnation of the Rendezvous went up in flames on Jan. 27, 1935. Within three months, another Rendezvous, bigger than before, was built on the site.

The beach frontage was increased to 216 feet. The interior was painted red and gray and decorated in a marine motif. Because of the Depression-era economy, the new structure was built at a fraction of the original building's price tag.

The ballroom at first featured house bands that included Bob Crosby (brother of Bing) and his Bobcats, Everett Hoagland and Gil Evans. But by the late '30s, the Rendezvous Ballroom became a major stop for national acts touring the West Coast.

The list of acts, which were often featured live on a national radio program, included such notables as Ozzie Nelson and Harriet Hilliard (before they were married and became TV sitcom stars), Guy Lombardo, Harry James, Gene Krupa, Ted Lewis, Artie Shaw, Kay Kyser and more.

Famous singers at the ballroom included Bing Crosby, the Andrews Sisters, June Christy, Mae Diggs and Nat King Cole.

In 1938 the ballroom was dubbed the "Queen of Swing" by Look magazine. The magazine featured color photos and an article that called it "a mecca for pleasure-seeking modern youth." It went on to say that "more than 5,000 cats and alligators" were "cutting a rug" on a typical summer evening.

The musical season lasted all summer long, though the Rendezvous would open for 10 days at Easter for the annual rites of "Bal Week," the spring break party named for the Balboa Peninsula. With more success, the Rendezvous began holding concerts on Friday and Saturday evening during the fall and winter months of 1939.

The popularity of the Rendezvous and its ocean-front location often drew Hollywood celebrities. Errol Flynn would moor his yacht at Christian's Hut and wander over to the ballroom, often in the company of Howard Hughes.

With the advent of World War II, Balboa became a "liberty town" and the ballroom's attendance peaked with local servicemen packing the place. On New Year's Eve, 1943, Benny Goodman and his orchestra played at the Rendezvous to overflow crowds.

But the Big Band sound began to fade after the war. In its place, a former Rendezvous house musician and Newport Beach resident Stan Kenton began playing a unique style of progressive jazz at the ballroom. While Kenton is considered an important jazz innovator today, his music precluded any attempts at dancing by Rendezvous regulars.

The ballroom changed hands several times in the early 50s. Kenton himself owned the hall for a time as part of a planned "rebirth of jazz." But no one drew the crowds like the Big Bands until the advent of Dick Dale and the surf sound in 1955.

Dale and his Deltones created a loud, propulsive music with electric guitars and amplifiers. Dale promoted his Rendezvous concerts at the local high schools until some 4,000 kids were showing up nightly during the summer.

And while Dale drove up the decibel level, the crowd would start a frenzied chain dance that became known as the "Surfer Stomp." His surf sound reached its pinnacle with the release of "Let's Go Trippin'" in 1961.

It would be the last great era at the Rendezvous. A band played music for the final time Aug. 6, 1966, the night before the ballroom's second and last fire. The band's name was, ironically, the Cindermen.

Today, the only reminder of the Rendezvous is a commemorative plaque at the corner of Washington and Ocean Front. It reads, "The music and dancing have ended, but the memories linger on."

The Rendezvous Ballroom saw several musical eras, from the Big Bands to rock 'n' roll.

STUDENTS RELIVE DAYS OF ONE-ROOM SCHOOLHOUSE

There should be a sign for the youngsters who enter the old El Toro Grammar School in Lake Forest: Leave your Nintendo at the door.

That's because when they step inside, they are transported to the turn-of-the-century, courtesy of the Living History program at Heritage Hill Park, a county regional park dedicated to preserving local history.

Staffed by volunteer retired schoolteachers, the Living History program introduces fourth-graders from Orange County schools to the educational experience of their great-grandparents.

The school building itself is the original El Toro Grammar School that was the only grade school in south county a hundred years ago. It's a classic one-room Victorian structure with a bell tower that looks like it's straight out of a Norman Rockwell painting.

The Living History program was designed by local historian Pat Eby. She conducted two years of research to make the experience authentic.

I visited the schoolhouse one recent morning as students from Capistrano Valley Christian School were donning vintage era clothing for their day in class. The girls wore pinafores and bonnets, while the boys put on vests and kerchiefs. Even their teacher and parent helpers were in early 1900s get-up.

Eleanor Smith, the "schoolmarm" for the day, greeted the students with a ring of the school tower bell.

"Once we are inside, the class will be taught as it would have been in 1903," Smith told the youngsters. "I will talk of current events from that era and you will be asked to stand when answering a question as students did in those days."

A schoolteacher's life was much different then, Smith explained. They arrived early to fire-up the pot-bellied stove, clean and fill the kerosene lamps and plan lessons for first through eighth grades. The teachers earned just $50 a month and lived with a family in town.

For their time-traveling class, the students assumed the names of pupils who actually attended the El Toro Grammar School. They were given information on what the student's life was like, the occupations of their fathers and the responsibilities of the mother at home.

The boys and girls filed in opposite doors as the class began. They remained standing and recited the Pledge of Allegiance just as it was written in 1892 by Francis Bellamy for National Public School Celebration Day.

Inside the schoolroom were eight separate blackboards, one for each of the different grades. In the back of the classroom was a display with photos of students from long ago and of Edna Nichols, the last schoolmarm back in 1914.

Smith began the class by talking about "current" events from 1903, including an upcoming presidential election and the wild personality of the one of the candidates — Teddy Roosevelt. She also noted the Wright Brothers' first flight that year, and the Model T's coming off the line at Ford Motor Company.

The schoolmarm then called roll and asked students to talk about their families a bit.

Their answers showed that most were the children of ranchers who walked a few miles to the school each day. Many never went to high school because they were needed by their families on the farms. Besides, the nearest secondary school was a long ride to Santa Ana.

The girls talked of sewing clothes and canning fruit with their mothers, while the boys described carrying water a half-mile to the ranchhouse, or helping their fathers break in a new horse.

Student "Madeline West," for instance, told the class how she helped her parents shear sheep on their ranch over the weekend and how she rode a mule to the school that morning.

Next, the schoolmarm handed out slates with chalk for penmanship practice. She promised the class they will be getting something new next year — their own inkwells and writing plumes at their desks. Computers were still far into the future.

The students were then let out for recess where they learned a new game — hoop 'n' stick relays. In this old-time game, students try to roll wooden barrel hoops with sticks and race each other across the schoolyard.

Back in the classroom the students worked on arithmetic story problems that centered around farm life. Next they were handed McGuffey Readers.

The books were used for years in American schools and featured stories that always end with a moral. Some of the story titles included "Try, Try Again," "Meddlesome Matty" and "Waste Not, Want Not."

Smith thanked the children for coming and dismissed them for the day. I asked a couple of students what they thought of the class.

"I liked it," said Brian Barbin. "I learned that kids worked hard just like their parents in those days."

"It was like Tom Sawyer," said Tyler Martin. "I think it would've been great to have a horse and go to school in my bare feet."

When asked if they would give up TV and computer games to live back then, both quickly said, "No way."

The El Toro Grammar School still stands at Heritage Hill Park in Lake Forest.

THE BOY SCOUT JAMBOREE OF 1953

Many Orange Countians may not realize that we were once invaded — by an army of Boy Scouts, that is.

Back in 1953 nearly 50,000 Scouts from all over the world made camp on sagebrush where Fashion Island stands today. Called the Boy Scout Jamboree, it was the largest meeting of Scouts up to that time.

Touted in the local newspaper as "the greatest assemblage of democratic youth in history," the Jamboree drew scores of celebrities from Hollywood, including Bob Hope, Mitzi Gaynor, Jimmy Stewart and Debbie Reynolds. Dale Evans, Roy Rogers and his horse Trigger put on a Western show. Even then-Vice President Richard Nixon stopped by to offer his greetings.

The event was forever memorialized in county history when the thoroughfare from the freeway to the coast was renamed Jamboree Road after the Scouts broke camp and returned home.

Two previous Scout Jamborees had been held in and around Washington D.C. in 1937 and 1950. However, those early incarnations didn't come close to matching the scope and size of the Orange County event.

The idea of a "jamboree" was started in Britain by Scout founder Lord Baden-Powell in 1913. The purpose was to test the leadership skills and knowledge the Scouts had acquired and show the world the Scouting ideals of international cooperation and goodwill.

William Spurgeon, an executive with The Irvine Co. and former Scout, was the force behind Orange County's selection as the site for the third Jamboree in the U.S. He approached Myford Irvine, owner of the Irvine ranch, to allow the Scouts to camp on his property.

Irvine took some time mulling over the prospect of 50,000 energetic youngsters camping on his land for a week. But in the end, he decided to let the Scouts use a 3,000-acre site overlooking Newport Bay rent-free. Irvine also agreed to spend $250,000 preparing "Jamboree City" for the massive influx of Scouts.

Nearly nine months before the first Scouts arrived, an Army Quonset hut appeared along Pacific Coast Highway as the event's construction headquarters. With the help of other local businesses, Jamboree City was built, complete with its own phone line, sewer system, 12 miles of water line and eight miles of road.

A shipment of 280 tons of Army tents arrived and were converted into telephone exchanges, trading posts, infirmaries, 5,000 troop kitchens, showers and more. More than 30,000 tents were placed throughout the site for the Scouts to erect as their sleeping quarters.

By July 13 Scouts began arriving from all parts of the U.S. in 100 specially designated trains. Scouts from 20 other countries made their way to the site by boat and by plane. In two days, the most populous city in Orange County had been formed, with another 100,000 visitors expected through the week.

Each troop built a gateway to mark its territory with a local icon. Boys from Orange County slept with a massive painted orange above their tent community, while Lone Star flags marked the Texas contingent and a replica of the Liberty Bell stood watch beside a troop from Philadelphia.

Scouts from Japan, Canada, Australia, Denmark and Mexico mingled with the U.S. kids. During this Cold War era, the Jamboree was considered a symbol of international friendship among Western nations.

By day the boys explored Southern California with field trips to Santa Catalina Island, Knott's Berry Farm and the Marine Corps base. The city of Huntington Beach closed off a mile of shoreline for the Scouts, where they were allowed to swim the waves in groups of 5,000.

Each evening the throng would converge on a massive amphitheater. They were entertained by film and stage stars or watched fellow Scouts show their skills in first aid, disaster work and physical fitness competitions.

For many of the youngsters, though, the highlight of the Jamboree wasn't on the schedule. Trading, a time-honored tradition among Boy Scouts, flourished in "swap tents."

As noisy as the Stock Exchange, the boys traded mementos from their hometowns. Everything was fair game, including pieces of rock from Alcatraz Island, lobster claws from Maine, frogs from Texas and abalone shells from local shores. State flags were also big trading items, and one boy accumulated most of them by trading rides on his unicycle.

As you might expect from growing youngsters, food was consumed in incredible quantities. More than 50,000 eggs, 36 miles worth of hot dogs, 620,000 quarts of milk and 169,000 loaves of bread were brought in on 90 freight cars. The amount of food eaten that week would have fed an average family of four for the next 500 years.

The Boy Scouts ended their time in Orange County with a Saturday night closing ceremony. The boys lit 50,000 candles and rededicated themselves to the Scout Oath of honoring God and country.

The last part of the ceremony featured a song written especially for the event:

There'll be long and dusty trails,
and good tall tales
Of how we got to California
We'll meet Scouts from everywhere,
our Scout songs will fill the air
at the Jamboree in California!

The Boy Scout Jamboree of 1953 drew nearly 50,000 Scouts.

Richard Halliburton, the Forgotten County Writer

Legendary writers of the past dot the California geography — Jack London of Oakland, John Steinbeck of the Central Valley, Raymond Chandler of Los Angeles...

But is there an author Orange County can call its own? One candidate would have to be Richard Halliburton, perhaps the most famous adventure writer of his time.

During the 1920s and 30s, Halliburton's books about his daring travels around the globe were giant best-sellers. In the era before TV and supersonic jets, his true-life narratives such as "The Royal Road to Adventure," "The Flying Carpet" and "Seven League Boots" captured the imagination of the American public.

After years of traveling, in 1937 Halliburton chose a desolate hill of sagebrush in Laguna Beach to settle down and build a house. It stands to this day, now hidden by development and forgotten to most countians.

Born to well-to-do parents near Memphis in 1900, Halliburton didn't have an interest in a life of traveling and adventure until his college days at Princeton. There he heard globe-trotting journalist Harry Franck describe far-away people and places, and Halliburton was hooked.

In 1921 he sailed to Europe, telling his parents, "I've gone to work. My trip is my occupation in life." He hoped to be a great intercontinental vagabond, seeing the world while producing travel articles for newspapers and magazines.

In Switzerland, Halliburton found guides that led him on a climb of the Matterhorn. A late-season storm nearly killed him along the way, but he was able to reach the summit, calling it "the fiercest moment of intense living I've ever experienced."

His travels continued in the Mideast, where he spent a night atop a pyramid in Egypt and swam across the Nile River. Moving on to India, he hid on the grounds of the Taj Mahal at night and swam in the giant reflecting pool.

He later stowed away on a ship bound for Singapore when pirates stole all his money and even his shoes. In Japan, after being told it had never been done, he made a mid-winter, solo ascent of Mt. Fuji.

After 50,000 miles and 600 days, Halliburton sailed home and headed for New York, determined to find a publisher for a book he was planning. There were no takers, so he began a speaking tour of schools and clubs. When he spoke at his alma mater of Princeton, a book editor at the Bobbs-Merrill Company was impressed. Halliburton got his book.

He called it "The Royal Road to Romance," and while it was still in production he was off again. This time he wanted to retrace the wanderings of the mythical Ulysses. He continued doing stunts, too, such as swimming the Strait of Dadanelles separating Asia from Europe.

He returned home by Christmas 1925 and, although receiving mixed reviews, his book was on the best-seller list. By the end of 1926 it had sold more than 100,000 copies, earning him $70,000 in royalties.

Halliburton was famous. Another best seller, "The Glorious Adventure," upped his speaking fee to $750. People packed auditoriums to see him, and he played the part of celebrity by always appearing in top hat and spats. Cecil B. De Mille even called to inquire about movie rights.

The daredevil stunts that pushed his book sales continued. He swam the length of the alligator-infested Panama Canal, flew an open cockpit plane up the face of Mt. Everest and jumped 70 feet into the Mayan "Well of Death" for newsreel photographers in the Yucatan.

He found time to write an adventure book for children called "The First Book of Marvels." He added a sequel and both books became a part of many people's childhood memories from the era.

After six novels and years of traveling, by the late '30s Halliburton was tiring of the globe-trotting lifestyle. He decided to attempt one last bold adventure — crossing the Pacific during peak typhoon season in a Chinese junk.

Between preparations for the death-defying stunt, he contracted architect Bill Alexander to build the Laguna Beach mansion. Constructed mostly of concrete with a spectacular view of the Pacific, the house included then-novel features as a garbage disposal, central heating and a dumb-waiter connecting the three floors.

The architecture was so innovative for its day that the house can still be classified as modern. Halliburton entertained Hollywood celebrities and dignitaries he had met during his travels at the home.

By 1939 he was ready to sail a Chinese junk called the Sea Dragon 9,000 miles to San Francisco. On March 3, the Halliburton expedition left Hong Kong.

On March 24, the ocean liner President Coolidge, 18,000 miles west of Hawaii and bucking 40-foot typhoon waves, picked up a radio message from the boat.

The message said, "Southerly gales... rain squall... lee rail under water... wet bunks... hard-tack... having wonderful time... wish you were here instead of me."

It was the last anyone ever heard from Richard Halliburton.

Today, his legend is kept alive in a library and archives dedicated to him at Rhodes College in his hometown of Memphis. A small but fervent following compare him to such fictional characters as Indiana Jones and Phileas Fogg of Jules Verne's "Around the World in 80 Days." Except Halliburton was real.

His Laguna Beach house stands as a reminder of the famous author who traveled the entire world but chose Orange County as his home.

Adventure writer Richard Halliburton

ALL RISE! THE CASE OF THE OLD COUNTY COURTHOUSE

The gothic-style Old Orange County Courthouse in the Santa Ana Civic Center has to be one of the more unique public buildings in the county, if not all of Southern California.

With its dark-red brick exterior and Medieval-like facade, it looks more like a set from a Stephen King movie than the courthouse that served Orange County's jurisprudence until 1979.

It's easy to imagine defendants coming to trial feeling anxious upon entering this foreboding structure. It could be that was exactly the reaction early county prosecutors wanted.

Like so much of Santa Ana history, the courthouse got its start with W.H. Spurgeon, the city's first mayor. In 1870, he set aside a piece of land where be believed a county courthouse would be built someday. It was a far-sighted move, considering the territory was still part of Los Angeles County at the time.

For years the lot lay vacant and was known as "Spurgeon Park," hosting such summertime events as an archery tournament, ox roasts, camp meetings and Fourth of July celebrations. Children from nearby Central School used it as a playground during the rest of the year.

After nearly 20 years of political wrangling and five failed attempts at incorporation, the lower third of Los Angeles County finally became Orange County in 1889.

Santa Ana emerged as the county seat, disappointing other hopefuls such as Anaheim and the City of Orange. One of the first points of business by the new county government was to erect a $4,000 three-cell lock-up in 1890.

Prisoners in the wood and brick jail had a pesky habit of digging their way to freedom through its walls, however. Sheet metal attached to the outer walls deterred prison breaks but failed to keep vigilantes from breaking in and hanging accused murderer Francisco Torres in 1892.

The board of supervisors began searching for a site big enough for a new jail. They selected the property Spurgeon had set aside 23 years earlier. Spurgeon sold them the land on the condition a county courthouse would be built on the site within 10 years.

The new jail, completed in 1897, was more intimidating than even the courthouse building is today. It featured four towers with conical roofs, numerous chimneys, spires and turrets that added to a fortress-like appearance. It survived until 1925, and was known by its residents as "Lacy's Hotel," named after county sheriff Theo Lacy.

In 1899, as the deadline of Spurgeon's 10-year condition drew near, a $100,000 bond issue was passed to fund construction of the courthouse. A call went out for a design competition. After the winner was found to have bribed some of the supervisors, red-faced officials chose the second-place finisher — architect C.L. Strange.

Strange's design for the courthouse was called "Richardson Romanesque," a style that became popular for civic structures after the Civil War.

Ground was broken in 1900. For the outer stonework, Strange had chosen beige-colored Chatsworth Park stone. But it was decided that red sandstone from Arizona would absorb less water and be easier to cut. With the substitution, the courthouse building took on a darker, more intimidating appearance.

Upon completion, the courthouse's outer dimensions measured 136 x 88 feet. Two stories were stacked on top of a basement, and a tower extended 135 feet above the ground, making it the highest man-made point in the county.

Officials had intended to include a clock in the tower, but a hefty $500 price tag encouraged them to let residents check their own pocket watches instead. The tower was dismantled after a 1933 earthquake damaged it beyond repair.

The interior was finished in solid oak, but officials substituted low-cost tile and granite instead of the planned marble floors. Only a grand staircase maintained its original design, with ornate Corinthian columns, red marble stairs and wrought-iron railings.

Many of the early well-known trials at the courthouse involved movie stars who were shooting films around the county, including Tom Mix, Douglas Fairbanks and William Russell. Most were taken in for speeding.

In 1921, silent film star Bebe Daniels spent 10 days behind bars for going 56 mph. The incident received national attention and was the subject of a story in the well-read Saturday Evening Post. She later starred in a movie about the incident titled "Too Much Speed."

Through the years, several celebrated cases received national attention at the courthouse. Among them was the case of Beulah Overell and her boyfriend George "Bud" Gollum, accused of dynamiting her parents to death aboard a yacht in Newport Harbor.

The longest trial on record at the courthouse was the McCracken child molestation and murder trial in 1951. It was also the first murder trial ever televised in California and shortly afterwards the California Judicial Council established regulations for media coverage.

An interesting historical sidelight is that Erle Stanley Gardner, author of the famous Perry Mason detective stories, attended many trials at the courthouse as a law student. In fact, his application for the bar exam was signed by a county Superior Court judge.

Although it originally housed every administrative office of the County of the Orange, the courthouse's occupants gradually transferred to newer spaces in the Civic Center through the years. By the late 70s, only a few trials were held inside the old building, and in 1979 the Old Orange County Courthouse held its last trial.

The old Orange County Courthouse before the earthquake of 1933 destroyed the tower.

Dr. Arnold O. Beckman: The Story of an Inventor

Decades before Orange County became the high-tech mecca it is today, there wasn't much around except cows and farms.

That started to change back in 1954 when Beckman Instruments, Inc., a scientific devices manufacturer, moved from Pasadena to settle on a 38-acre Fullerton orange grove. Its worldwide headquarters remains at that very site to this day.

The company's founding genius was Arnold Orville Beckman, a Caltech chemistry professor turned entrepreneur. Dr. Beckman today is 96, alive and well and living in Corona del Mar. Company officials say he still reads a newspaper every day, surfs the Internet and occasionally offers an idea or two to young people entering science.

It is ideas that made Dr. Beckman such a huge success. He is considered one of the top five inventors of scientific instruments, creating devices that revolutionized the study and understanding of human biology, ultimately saving countless lives around the world. He is a member of the Inventor's Hall of Fame, along with the likes of Thomas Edison and Alexander Bell.

Beckman was born in 1900 in Cullom, a tiny farming community in Illinois. On his 10th birthday, his father built him an 8 x 10-foot shed and gave him a set of tools to learn blacksmithing. A few weeks late, however, the young Beckman discovered a book in the family attic that changed his life.

It was called Steele's "Fourteen Weeks in Chemistry." Published in 1861, it contained instructions for carrying out simple experiments using ordinary chemicals. Beckman was intrigued, and he turned his birthday shed into a rudimentary chemistry lab.

Before he was in his teens, Beckman landed a job as a "chemist" — analyzing the butter content of cream at a local dairy. In high school, he convinced school officials to allow him to take chemistry classes at a nearby college. By the time he graduated, he had accumulated two and a half years of college chemistry.

Beckman put himself through school and helped support his family by playing piano at silent movies (he learned to play after a half-dozen lessons.) After earning a master's degree in physical chemistry, Beckman was offered several scholarships for doctoral studies. He chose the California Institute of Technology, a new college at the time.

After a year at Caltech, Beckman was having a tough time living off the scholarship money. He decided to take a job offer at Bell Laboratories in New York, where his future wife Mabel Meinzer lived. At Bell, Beckman worked closely with electronics engineers, soaking up their knowledge and expertise.

In 1925 Caltech offered him a teaching assistantship. Mabel and Arnold were married and moved to California. Beckman resumed his doctoral studies while teaching general chemistry.

While the young professor taught, an inventor's imagination began to take hold. Beckman kept a journal and during these early years he wrote down ideas for inventions such as an electronic organ, a timing device for coffee percolators, and push-button car windows.

One day a chemist with the California Fruit Growers Exchange approached Beckman. His firm was having trouble measuring the acidity of lemon juice when combined with a preservative.

With his limited electronics knowledge, Beckman was able to sketch out the components and circuitry of his pH meter. It was designed to measure the acidity or alkalinity of any solution containing water, from drinking water to mud.

The chemist's colleagues kept borrowing the meter, which made Beckman wonder about selling the device. A market survey company told him he might sell 600 over 10 years, yet Beckman's instincts told him different. He ended up selling more than 400,000 units.

So began Beckman's "scientific appliances" company. He called his firm National Technical Laboratories, moved into a warehouse in Pasadena and left his teaching position.

Following the success of the pH meter, the company introduced the DU Spectrophotometer in 1941. Able to make a "fingerprint" of lab tests by measuring colors or wavelengths of light, the device has been called the scientific equivalent of the Model T.

An oxygen analyzer was developed in 1943, which immediately found an important application as a means to measure oxygen in incubators for premature babies. High oxygen contents had been causing blindness in some infants.

In the post-war years, the company raged ahead. In 1950, NTL became Beckman Instruments, Inc. and in 1952 made its first public stock offerings. By the early 50s, it had far out-grown its warehouse walls.

Beckman and a company official decided to scout land in the farm country of Orange County. They agreed on purchasing a huge site, more than they believed they would need, near the intersection of Harbor and Imperial Highway. A state-of-the-art facility was opened in 1954.

Today the $930-million company has 35 facilities worldwide and operates in more than 120 countries. Of its 6,200 employees, more than 2,500 are employed at Beckman's Fullerton and Brea sites.

Beckman Instruments, Inc. has made everything from a "rock smasher" for a Mars robot mission to an electronic shark repellent.

However, the company has never strayed very from Dr. Beckman's original focus on "the chemistry of life," and continues as a worldwide developer of hospital and bio-research lab systems.

And to think it all began with a 10-year-old boy and a book on chemistry.

Dr. Arnold Beckman with his pH meter

READ ALL ABOUT IT!
THE OC REGISTER STORY

From Lindbergh's flight to the mission to Mars, The Orange County Register has brought the news of the day to county residents for more than 90 years.

While news stories have come and gone, longtime readers of The Register may still remember the paper's irascible publisher — Raymond Cyrus (R.C.) Hoiles.

Hoiles, who died in 1970 at age 91, was the last of the fiercely independent newpaper publishers, infusing The Register's editorial pages with a personal Libertarian philosophy that often antagonized readers.

The irony today is that many of Hoiles' ideas once considered "crackpot" by some are now mainstream points of discussion, such as the privatization of schools, the legalization of drugs and limited government bureaucracy.

Hoiles was born in 1878 to a well-to-do farming family in Alliance, Ohio and began working at his brother Frank's hometown newspaper while attending college. Hoiles later worked as business manager and purchased one-third interest in the publication.

In 1919 R.C. and his brother purchased the Lorain Times Herald. R.C. held two-thirds interest and became the paper's publisher. Hoiles later sold his interest in the Alliance after his brother refused to run anti-union editorials.

In 1927 Hoiles purchased the Bucyrus Telegraph Forum, placing his son Clarence in charge, and bought another paper in Mansfield. Hoiles was on his way to becoming a successful publisher until 1928 when he became embroiled in one of the most bitter newspaper battles in the history of Ohio journalism.

Hoiles' Lorain newspaper had run an expose about a road construction firm illegally receiving a city contract. After the story hit the streets, the construction firm set out to ruin Hoiles. The firm began publishing a competing paper of its own in Lorain, then started another in Mansfield.

Then came the bombings. First, a bomb exploded on the front porch of the Hoiles home in November 1928. No one was injured and no suspects were caught. In September 1929 Hoiles experienced car trouble and went to a mechanic who discovered an undetonated bomb in the motor.

Hoiles purchased a bullet-proof car equipped with an engine lock and hired an armed guard to ride along with him. But with the increasingly intense competition for circulation and advertising dollars from the other newspapers, Hoiles decided to sell his papers to a large Ohio publisher in 1932.

During the next three years, Hoiles stayed out of the newspaper business, spending his time reading and fine-tuning his growing Libertarian philosophy. He believed that the daily newspaper was still the best outlet he could have to communicate his views.

So in 1935, when J. Frank Burke offered to sell Hoiles the Santa Ana Register, R.C. saw his opportunity, bought the paper and moved to California.

The Register traced its roots to The Evening Blade, first published in 1886 by "Uncle Billy" Spurgeon, the founder of Santa Ana. In 1905, Fred Unholz and Frank Ormer established a competing hometown paper, the Santa Ana Register. Losing the readership battle, the Blade merged with the Register in 1918.

When Hoiles purchased the Santa Ana Register, located at Third and Sycamore, it was the county's leading newspaper in circulation with 12,000 readers. Hoiles made his son Clarence co-publisher. Clarence would run the business side of things, while R.C. would take part in his favorite pastime — raising people's ire.

On Nov. 22, 1935, Hoiles published a statement to his readers, stating, "We would like to have the Register be a medium of helping Orange County citizens make our county a leader in social and ethical thought, raising our standard of living and helping spread sound thinking throughout the land."

The "sound thinking" Hoiles was referring to was his Libertarian credo of limited government and personal freedom, culled from his readings of various writers and philosophers, from Baruch Spinoza and John Locke to Henry David Thoreau and Ayn Rand.

R.C. became known as "The Sage of Sycamore" with his caustic columns against almost all forms of government control. He saved his most venomous attacks for the tax-supported "gun-run" schools.

People often interpreted his editorials as being anti-education, but that really wasn't the case, according to many who knew Hoiles. He believed only that students would be better served by private institutions. He even offered money to any public school teacher or superintendent to debate him, but few dared to.

Hoiles' other controversial stands on unions, prostitution, the draft and other issues often resulted in a loss of subscribers, but that didn't deter him.

"It was hard to sell ads sometimes when you spent so much time fighting philosophical arguments," recalled one advertising rep. "Every day there was something 60 percent of the people disagreed with."

During World War II Hoiles' ideas about personal freedom led him to take a courageous stand against the internment of Japanese-Americans. He was the only major newspaper publisher in the country to criticize the U.S. government policy.

Hoiles' against-the-grain approach didn't slow the paper's success. With the business acumen of his son, C.H., the Register flourished. Today it serves more than 400,000 readers and boasts one of the largest classified advertising sections in the country.

Freedom Communications, Inc., started by the Hoiles in 1950, became a diversified media company with 26 daily newspapers, six broadcast TV stations and 18 consumer and trade magazines.

Defying all convention, R.C. Hoiles had become an astounding publishing success. He was named to the California Newspaper Hall of Fame in 1979.

The original Santa Ana Register building at Third and Sycamore

SAN CLEMENTE: A SPANISH VILLAGE INVENTED BY 'OLE'

With its Spanish name and architecture, I had always assumed San Clemente was founded by Spanish missionaries, like so many of the other great California cities.

In reality, this picturesque seaside town was created almost single-handedly during the 1920s by Ole Hanson, the son of Norwegian immigrants. Well-known to many San Clemente residents, Hanson's name probably doesn't ring too many bells among the vast majority of Orange Countians.

Hanson was born in a log cabin in Wisconsin in 1874. His parents had traveled from Norway to the U.S. to take advantage of the Homestead Act, when the government was giving away land free to anyone wanting to farm it.

A bright youngster, Hanson was teaching in a rural schoolhouse by age 13. He began studying law as a teenager and passed the state bar exam at age 19, having to wait until he was 21 to practice.

In 1904 Hanson was in a train wreck and suffered partial paralysis in one leg for the rest of his life. That didn't stop him from traveling West in two flatbed wagons with his young family, with Hanson walking most of the 2,800 miles to Seattle.

There in the bustling young city Hanson quickly gained success. He purchased a grocery store, sold real estate and built a house for his family. Next came politics, and Hanson vigorously campaigned against gambling and vice to win a seat in the state legislature. After his term was up, he was elected mayor of Seattle.

Following World War I, Hanson was lured to California by tales of undeveloped land and a growing population. He opened a real estate office in Los Angeles and built 2,000 tract homes on Slauson Avenue.

After seeing the beautiful coastline between Los Angeles and San Diego during a sailing trip, Hanson's heart was set on building a "Spanish village by the sea."

In 1924 he purchased 2,000 acres on the Orange County coast and set out to make his dream a reality. At first he wanted to call the community "Cabrillo" after the European discoverer of California, but then he learned the tiny island off the coast had been named by Spanish explorers for St. Clement.

So he called the hills of sagebrush overlooking the Pacific Ocean "San Clemente," and was inspired to write a friend:

"I can see hundreds of white-walled homes bonneted with red tile. I want plazas, playgrounds, schools, clubs, swimming pools, a golf course, a fishing pier and a beach enlivened with people getting a healthy joy out of life."

"I have a clean canvas five miles long and one and one-half miles wide, and I am determined to paint a clean picture."

Teaming up with Los Angeles millionaire Hamilton Cotton to develop the land, Hanson pitched a large tent and presented his dream to 600 prospective buyers on Dec. 6, 1925. On that day he sold $125,000 worth of San Clemente property. Within six months, he sold 1,200 lots.

But Hanson was not the typical real estate developer of the time looking to make a quick killing — he wanted to start a community. He ensured that future residents would comply with his dream for the city by writing rules into their deeds of ownership.

First, no one could purchase the land for speculation — only buyers planning to build were allowed. Next, all construction had to pass his architectural review board which ensured the exterior of every building, whether a home, gas station or lumber yard, incorporated red tile roofs and white stucco walls.

Also, no building could exceed four stories and every business sign had to receive approval to maintain unobstructed ocean views.

Hanson kept his end of the bargain by first deeding 3,000 feet of beachfront to residents. He also constructed the fishing pier at a cost of $70,000 and sold it to the city for one dollar. Then Hanson built and donated a hospital, schoolhouse, community clubhouse, swimming pool and more to the new community.

When news of Hanson's project first hit the papers, most Southern Californians thought he was crazy to build a town so far away from the two major metropolitan areas of Los Angeles and San Diego.

But just two years later a Los Angeles Times columnist wrote, "If the charms of this place could be shown to the poor, snow-bound, wind-beaten people back East, there would be an exodus so great the hills above San Clemente would be covered like mushrooms."

Hanson built himself a fine, Spanish-style villa overlooking the sea that became known as Casa Romantica. As national finance director for the Democratic Party, he entertained Franklin D. Roosevelt there in 1935. (President Nixon took up residence in H.H. Cotton's mansion overlooking the ocean during his administration.)

Hanson died in 1940 and, with no one left to enforce the Spanish-style building code, the city started to lose its distinctive look. But roughly 250 Ole Hanson homes still stand in San Clemente, as well as many of the civic structures he donated to the city.

A bust of Hanson sits outside the Casa Romantica, a reminder to all of the Norwegian-American who built a Spanish village by the sea.

Ole Hanson, founder of San Clemente

MUCKENTHALER CENTER - HOME TO THE ARTS IN NORTH OC

A Mediterranean-style mansion on a hill of rolling lawns in Fullerton, the Muckenthaler Cultural Center is North Orange County's cultural oasis.

Known affectionately as "the Muck" by patrons, the center is home to a smorgasbord of cultural events, including art exhibitions, jazz and classical concerts, outdoor plays and an annual "Imagination Celebration" that introduces children to the world of art.

But one question has always risen in my mind whenever I hear of the center — who exactly were the Muckenthalers?

I discovered their story is a tale of a man and woman from two worlds — Walter Muckenthaler, the son of German immigrants, and Adella Kraemer, a descendant of the county's oldest Spanish ranch family.

Walter's family emigrated to the U.S. in the mid-19th century from a small village in Germany known as Muggenthaler. They became Kansas farmers and in 1909 a son, Albert, moved to the German community of Anaheim with his young family.

His son Walter grew up in the idyllic Orange County world of orange groves and trips to the beach. He graduated from Anaheim High School and went to work as a city engineer for Fullerton after receiving a degree from Cal Berkeley.

Adella's mother was Angelina Yorba, a member of the original Spanish rancho family. One of nine children, Adella grew up in the prim and proper tradition of a Spanish heiress.

Walter met Adella at a dance at St. Boniface Catholic Church in Anaheim. The two began a courtship that was somewhat controversial for its day because of the different cultural backgrounds. The couple was married in the early morning hours of a weekday to avoid the disapproving eyes of the community.

The newlyweds purchased an 80-acre orange grove in Fullerton, which included a eight-acre hill site for their dream home. Walter enlisted architect Frank Benchley to draw the plans, who had recently built the California Hotel in Fullerton.

Walter had seen a Mediterranean-style building at Balboa Park in San Diego. Walter told Adella he wanted to build a "a house for a sunlit land."

Built in 1924 at a cost of $35,000, the 18-room mansion was designed in the Italian Renaissance style, with white stucco walls and red tile roof. The home was an immediate stand-out from other homes in the area.

The house featured windows and accompanying balconies at every turn. Standing on the cast stone balcony off the upstairs bedroom, Walter and Adella could easily view Catalina Island on cloudless days.

An octagonal solarium was built to the right of the main door, featuring eight floor-to-ceiling windows and a chandelier in the center. On the left side of the entry was an arched doorway that led to a living room with a massive tiled fireplace. Another fireplace was placed between the formal dining room and Walter's library.

A staircase with Italian wrought-iron railing led visitors to an upstairs bedroom that overlooked a large patio area with an open-air atrium. Surrounding the patio was a maid's room, screened porch, a gardener's room, garage, office and two downstairs bedrooms.

Along the patio wall was an oil mural depicting a Spanish señorita in the foreground with a view of a castle and Spanish countryside.

Landscaping around the impressive home took four years, and included a fountain, palm trees, an avocado grove and rare trees.

The Muckenthaler home was a masterpiece of design that seemed to perfectly complement its Southern California environment. Instead of copying the Midwestern farmhouse, it set the stage for a new era of homes and business structures built in its style.

Walter died in 1958 after a long illness. Adella Muckenthaler stayed in the home until 1964. She and their only child, Harold, deeded the hilltop home to the City of Fullerton in 1965 as a gift to the city.

Walter had been an avid amateur illustrator his entire life, and the family stipulated that the house and grounds could only be used as a cultural center for the entire community.

While languishing for a time due to lack of funding, the home was fully restored in 1982 with track lighting and movable walls added for art exhibitions. A kitchen outfitted with restaurant-sized appliances was added for receptions, luncheons and fund-raisers.

The Muckenthaler features an eclectic mix of art exhibitions. This year, for instance, the center displayed Russian Socialist propaganda art, paintings showcasing the history of the automobile, and more than 2,500 works of Fullerton school children.

An outdoor amphitheater was added in 1991 and features a variety of concerts and stage plays. This year the center's Theatre on the Green program featured a murder mystery from Broadway and a hit comedy from London.

The arts center with the distinctive name has become a favorite gathering place for residents in North Orange County.

The Muckenthaler Center in Fullerton

HOW DISNEY CHOSE OC FOR HIS NEW LAND

Is there any place in the U.S. recognized by more people around the world than Disneyland?

For more than 40 years the amusement park has drawn visitors young and old from every country who journey to experience the childhood pleasures evoked at the Anaheim landmark.

Those of us who have lived in the county for years tend to be blasé about the park. Yet recently I drove by Disneyland and saw families excitedly taking pictures in front of the sign with the familiar slogan, "The Happiest Place on Earth," a reminder of the fondness people still hold for the park.

How did this all-American institution land in a county orange grove? Cartoonist Walt Disney needed a place big enough for his dreams, and a mystery man named Fred Wallich stepped in to help.

As a young father, Disney had observed his two small daughters enjoying themselves at amusement parks designed solely for children. That inspired Disney to conceive of a place where everyone in the family — children, parents and grandparents — could participate and have fun together.

His original ideas took the shape of a "magical little park" which he proposed to build on two acres next to his Disney Studios in Burbank. The plan called for singing waterfalls and statues of Mickey Mouse, Donald Duck and other famous Disney characters from his movie cartoons.

One Disney Studios artist, later assigned to the original team of Disneyland designers, recalled his first memories of a Disney amusement park:

"I lived on Riverside Drive in Burbank in the '40s near the studio. I remember several Sundays seeing Walt across the street in a weed-filled lot, standing, visualizing, all by himself."

"He would come to work on Monday and tell us about his plans. But the longer Walt thought about the park, the more ideas he got and suddenly the weed-filled lot just wasn't big enough."

Disney's ideas became so ambitious he commissioned the Stanford Research Institute to find an ideal location for his park — one that could be purchased at a reasonable price from one owner, offer easy freeway access and was at least 100 acres.

The search was on. The Stanford scientists studied several sites in Southern California, considering such factors as climate (including rain, fog, humidity and wind), population growth and access to utility lines.

The only site researchers studied in Orange County was a La Mirada ranch. But, according to Earnest Moeller, the Anaheim Chamber of Commerce director at the time, it took an unsolicited letter from Fred Wallich to focus their attention on Anaheim. Wallich wrote to the Stanford team about a field of orange groves in Anaheim.

"This site," Wallich wrote,"was not found on your search through Orange County records because there are 17 parcels involving many owners. Yet I know many of the owners are considering selling to a housing subdivision."

Wallich went on to say the site abutted the construction of the Santa Ana Freeway, which was scheduled for completion in less than a year, giving Disneyland excellent freeway access.

To this day it is a mystery who Mr. Wallich was. Several Anaheim city officials later guessed he was a realtor or developer who lived outside Orange County but had knowledge of county real estate.

The researchers discovered the 160-acre orange grove fit all their criteria. The team concluded the area would be the center of population for the Los Angeles basin in coming years. Their prediction was amazingly accurate — the center of population today for the eight Southern California counties is Fullerton, four miles from Disneyland.

"I first saw the site for Disneyland back in 1953," Disney said. "In those days it was all flat land - no rivers, no mountains, no castles or rocket ships - just orange groves and a few acres of walnut trees."

After purchasing the site, Disney's ideas for the park continued to evolve. Many said his plans were becoming too expensive. Disney decided to risk nearly all his fortune to see his dream realized, which included selling his vacation home in Palm Springs and borrowing against his life insurance policy.

Ground was broken for Disneyland on July 21, 1954. It was predicted by observers that the venture would be a "Hollywood spectacular" — a spectacular failure. After all, there had never been an amusement park that had the high standards Disney promised for his Magic Kingdom. And no "kiddie" park had ever come close to Disney's investment of $17 million.

Amusement park operators around the country agreed that Disneyland would not have enough ride capacity, too much of the park would not produce revenue, and the planned attractions would cost too much to maintain.

Just one year later on July 17, 1955, Disney opened the gates to his new creation. Nearly 30,000 guests (the entire Anaheim population at the time) and a live national TV audience of 90 million witnessed the opening. Emceeing the ABC-TV special were Art Linkletter, Bob Cummings and an actor named Ronald Reagan.

True to Disney's predictions, the park saw immediate acceptance, welcoming its one-millionth guest after just seven weeks of operation. People were enchanted by the themed lands and rides, the opportunity to mingle with life-size Disney cartoon characters, and see bygone days revived such as a horse-drawn streetcar on a small-town Main Street.

One enthusiastic critic described Disneyland this way: "Disney has taken an area of activity — the amusement park — and lifted it to a standard so high in its performance and in its respect for people, he has really created a brand-new thing."

Disneyland's total guest attendance is now nearing 300 million, and has included everyone from Emperor Hirohito to Michael Jackson. Today the park is planning a $1.4-billion expansion, which should give people even more reason to visit "the happiest place on earth."

Walt Disney and Mickey Mouse tour Anaheim's magical park.

ACKNOWLEDGEMENTS

The author would like to thank the following people and organizations for their research, photos and assistance:

First American Title Insurance Company in Santa Ana, Calif. (especially Jacque Gates, Barbara Blankman and Kathy Snyder); Anne Harder, Santa Ana Public Library history room; historian Jim Sleeper; Diann Marsh, Santa Ana Historical Preservation Society; The Orange County Register; The Los Angeles Times; Creighton Hunter; Nathan Reed; Bud Anderson, Costa Mesa Historical Society; Shannon Tucker, Orange Old Towne Preservation Society; The Irvine Company; Barbara Milkovich, Huntington Beach Historical Society; Ellen K. Lee, Helena Modjeska Foundation; Lisa Babilonia-Jones, Ralph B. Clark Interpretive Center; Vi Smith, Martin Aviation; Jane Newell, Anaheim Public Library history room; Ruth Wardwell, Chapman University; Bill Short, The Burrows Library, Rhodes College in Memphis; Chris Ragon, St. Catherine's Military School in Anaheim; Brian Langston, Bowers Museum; Knott's Berry Farm; Ann Beasley, Huntington Beach International Surfing Museum; Joleen Parham, Balboa Bay Club; the Muckenthaler Center; Los Alamitos Race Course; Orange County Fair & Exposition Center; Beckman Instruments, Inc.; Richard Smith; Cathy Thomas, Fullerton Public Library history room; Heritage Hill Historical Park; Jim Graves, Mission San Juan Capistrano; El Toro Marine Corps Air Base; Steve Donaldson, Orange County Railway Historical Society; Jackie Dooley, Special Collections, UCI Libraries; Betsy Vigus, Orange County Historical Society; and to everyone I may have missed.

And a special thanks to Joe MacPherson, for his interest in history and his desire to share his love of Orange County's colorful past.